southwest usa
road atlas + travel guide

CONTENTS

Travel Guide

The following 32 pages should help you maximize your on-the-road time. **Driving tours** for 7 regions of the Southwest, plus itineraries for its major cities, highlight points of interest rated according to the **Michelin star system:**

> ★★★ **Highly recommended**
> ★★ **Recommended**
> ★ **Interesting**

In addition to the Atlas pages, **customized maps** in the Travel Guide complement the driving tours.

Abbreviations: E (east), S (south), N (north), SW (southwest), etc. Mi (miles), Sq Ft (square feet), CVB (Convention and Visitors Bureau), No. (street address number).

Most tours includes **Bed and Board,** a brief description of popular **restaurants** and interesting **places to stay** categorized by price. Price ranges for lodging reflect the average cost for a standard double room (2 people) per night in high season, not including tax. For restaurants, rates indicate the average cost of an appetizer, an entrée and dessert for one person, not including beverages, tax or gratuity.

Taos Pueblo,
New Mexico

Lodging Tips

Advance Reservations

Reserve accommodations well in advance of your trip. Before you go, check the establishment's Web site for special packages or seasonal discounts and find out the cancellation policy. Check travel Web sites that specialize in hotel discounts such as quikbook.com, travelocity.com, orbitz.com. and others. Always ask the establishment what discounts are available: automobile club membership, senior citizen, military personnel, etc.

On-site Bookings

If you prefer **impromptu stays,** phone or check the Web site of the local tourist information office well in advance to determine peak tourist season and festivals or other events taking place when you plan to be there. Graduation ceremonies, a big football game or parents' day in a college town can fill up area lodging a year in advance. Upon arrival, stop at the tourism office to get help with local accommodations.

Practical information such as driving and parking regulations, visitor information and shopping venues is included for the major cities.

For comprehensive coverage of the landscape, history, culture and attractions of the Southwestern USA, see the Michelin **GREEN GUIDE USA WEST,** *the ultimate guidebook for the independent traveler, as well as the* **CALIFORNIA ROAD ATLAS + TRAVEL GUIDE.**

Red Rock Country/Grand Canyon ★★★

If any single geographical feature symbolizes the United States in the minds of world travelers, it is Arizona's Grand Canyon. This 1,904sq-mi national park, located entirely in northwestern Arizona, extends from Lees Ferry, west to the Grand Wash Cliffs. Waters from seven western states drain into the mighty Colorado River, 1,450mi long from its source in Colorado's Rocky Mountains to Mexico's Gulf of California.

Some 80mi southeast of the South Rim is cool and mountainous Flagstaff, the region's biggest city. Nearby are the world's largest stand of ponderosa pines and Arizona's tallest mountains—the San Francisco Peaks, rising to 12,633ft at Humphreys Peak. The 30mi drive south from Flagstaff to Sedona, descending from 7,000ft to 4,500ft through the diverse forests and famed red-rock scenery of Oak Creek Canyon, is brief but captivating. Sedona has lured artists and other creative types for a century; in recent decades, the influx has included New Age devotees who claim to be drawn by a mystical energy ascribed to the rocks. Located in the Sonoran Desert, greater Phoenix is known as the Valley of the Sun. This desert oasis stretches across more than 2,000sq mi and takes in Scottsdale and other communities surrounding the relatively young urban center of Phoenix. *Note: The drive described below is divided into two tours, each routed from south to north (Phoenix to the Grand Canyon).*

Tour 1

Phoenix–Sedona–Flagstaff
222 miles   *Maps pages 4, 8–9 and Atlas pages 18, 29*

The tour begins in **Phoenix★**, one of eight US cities with major-league baseball, basketball, football and ice hockey teams. Several museums are on or near North Central Ave., a boulevard lined with palm, mesquite and palo verde trees, running north from the city hub, **Patriots Square** (Washington and Jefferson Sts., and Central Ave). Main streets are laid parallel in 1mi-by-1mi grids, making orientation and navigation simple. Revitalization east of the square has made **Civic Plaza** a major cultural center, site of **symphony hall** and **Herberger Theater**.
Heritage and Science Park (N. 5th, N. 7th, E. Washington and E. Monroe Sts.) contains **Heritage Square**, the **Arizona Science Center★** and the **Phoenix Museum of History★**.
Not to be missed is **The Heard Museum★★★** (2301 N. Central Ave.; take Washington St. W, turn right onto Central Ave.), devoted to Native American culture and art, especially Southwest tribes. This fine museum has amassed some 32,000 works of art, including baskets, jewelry, pottery, tex-tiles, painting, sculpture and nearly 500 hand-carved Hopi kachinas. Another highlight is the **Desert Botanical Garden★★** in Papago Park (1201 N. Galvin Pkwy.; from the Heard Museum, go 3 blocks S on Central Ave., turn left onto McDowell Rd., then right on 64th St. for .5mi.). This unique garden contains more than 20,000 desert plants, including cacti and succulents. Themed trails snake through the natural landscape, educating visitors along the way.

Hopi Kachina Dolls, The Heard Museum

Practicalities

Visitor Information

Phoenix CVB, 400 E. Van Buren St., Suite 600. 602-254-6500 or 877-225-5749. www.phoenixcvb.com. Visitor information centers at 50 N. 2nd St. (downtown) and Biltmore Fashion Park (2025 E. Camelback Rd.).

Shopping

Copper Square (downtown, Civic Plaza): 10 blocks of national retailers, specialty shops and restaurants. **Arizona Center** (downtown at Van Buren & 3rd Sts.): women's fashion, specialty shops, food court. **Biltmore Fashion Park** (E. Camelback Rd. off Rte. 51): upscale center with Saks Fifth Ave., Betsey Johnson, Talbots, specialty boutiques, restaurants. **Scottsdale Fashion Square** (Camelback & Scottsdale Rds.): 225 stores including Neiman Marcus, Nordstrom, specialty shops, restaurants, cinemas. **Paradise Valley Mall** (Cactus & Tatum Blvd.): major departments stores, Ann Taylor, Brookstone, Gap, specialty shops, eateries, cinema.

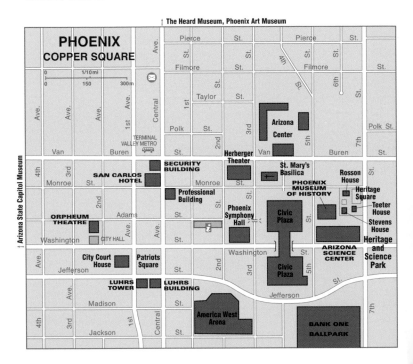

Bed and Board Phoenix

Lodging

Royal Palms Hotel and Casitas – *5200 E. Camelback Rd. / 602-840-3610. Over $300.* An intimate and secluded resort at the foot of Camelback Mountain, Royal Palms was built in Spanish Colonial style in 1929 as the gracious summer estate of a cruise-line executive. Guests now approach along a driveway lined with regal palm trees. The original mansion houses highly regarded **T. Cook's** *(over $50)*, serving Mediterranean-style cuisine.

Hotel San Carlos – *202 N. Central Ave. / 602-253-4121. $75-$125.* A yellow-brick downtown classic since 1928, the San Carlos is a historic anomaly in a region of spa resorts and golf haciendas. The lobby's chandeliers and period wallpaper give an Old World ambience; the rooftop pool is a modern amenity. **Seamus McCaffrey's Irish Pub** *($15-$30)* offers traditional pub fare.

Restaurants

Arizona Kitchen – *300 Wigwam Blvd. at The Wigwam Resort, Litchfield Park. Dinner only. Closed Sun-Mon. $30-$50. Southwestern.* Native American accents apply to cuisine and decor at this west Phoenix favorite. Blue-corn duck burritos, quail with pomegranate molasses glaze, and buffalo sirloin with a vanilla-bean chili sauce are highlights. Pottery and hand-woven place mats add to the mood.

Alice Cooper'stown – *101 E. Jackson St. 602-253-7337. $15-$30. American.* Two halls of fame—baseball and rock 'n' roll—coexist at this lively sports bar and grill near Bank One Ballpark.

While delivering barbecue and "fields of greens," servers wear black eye makeup in tribute to owner Alice Cooper, the Phoenix native famed as a musician.

Drive north from **Phoenix★** on I-17 to Exit 298 and take Rte. 179 N to **Sedona★★**, a small city in the heart of **Red Rock Country★★★**. Part resort town, part artist colony and part New Age center, Sedona attracts a hosts of visitors, many seeking spiritual enlightenment. Just north of the "Y" intersection on Rte. 89A, a plethora of shops and galleries in Old West-style structures offer everything from Native American crafts to New Age items. Down the hill on Route 179 sits **Tlaquepaque Arts & Crafts Village**, a charming shopping complex modeled after the village (40 specialty shops, galleries, and 4 restaurants).

Red Rock Country

Bed and Board *Sedona*

Lodging
L'Auberge de Sedona – *301 L'Auberge Ln. / 928-282-1661. $200-$300.* The main lodge's huge rolling logs and stone columns blend into the chiseled buttes and spires of Sedona's geology. The 33 cottages, on the other hand, have a country-French feel. Eleven acres of botanical gardens are joined to the award-winning creekside **L'Auberge Restaurant** *($30-$50)* by paths that wind past fruit trees and lilacs.

Enchantment Resort – *520 Boynton Canyon Rd. / 928-282-2900. $200-$300.* Low-profile, adobe-style casitas, with beehive fireplaces and private balconies, are nestled in the red rocks of Boynton Canyon. The spa offers restorative Native American earth-clay wraps. Diners enjoy rack of lamb with a pistachio crust at the award-winning

Yavapai Restaurant *($30-$50)*, which has a 180-degree view.

Restaurants
The Heartline Cafe – *1610 W. US-89A. / 928-282-0785. $30-$50. Creative Regional.* Named for the Zuni bear fetish symbolizing health, long life and good luck, this eclectic but highly regarded restaurant has won regional acclaim. Menu items include tea-smoked duck salad, sautéed Cajun shrimp and pistachio-crusted chicken.

René at Tlaquepaque – *Rte. 179 at Oak Creek. / 928-282-9225. $30-$50. Continental.* An institution in the Tlaquepaque Arts & Crafts Village, René is famed for its baked French onion soup and its signature rack of lamb, carved tableside. Other favorites are Dover sole, sweet-potato ravioli, and flambéed cherries jubilee.

To experience Red Rock Country up close, you'll need sturdy hiking boots or a four-wheel-drive vehicle. Several companies provide off-road Jeep tours to vista points, vortices, wildflower meadows, Sinagua ruins and other sites. If you are driving yourself, the formations are best accessed by four-wheel-drive vehicle via 12mi **Schnebly Hill Road★** (off Rte. 179, across Oak Creek bridge from the Rte.

89A "Y" junction), which offers splendid **views★★★**.

Leave Sedona on Rte. 89A, heading N to begin a 14mi scenic drive of **Oak Creek Canyon★★**—a 1,200ft-deep gorge that descends 2,500ft down the southern escarpment of the vast Colorado Plateau. Continue N on Rte. 89A and I-17 to **Flagstaff★**, nestled at the foot of the San Francisco Peaks, crowned by 12,633ft Humphreys Peak. This city serves as the commercial hub for a huge and sparsely populated area. From the visitor center in the 1926 Tudor Revival **railway station** (1 E. Rte. 66 at Leroux St.), walking tours depart for the downtown **historic district**, a highlight of which is the 1889 Hotel Weatherford (23 N. Leroux St.). Seven sandstone structures on the **Northern Arizona University** campus (Kendrick St. & Ellery Ave., S of Butler Ave.), built between 1894 and 1935, are

on the National Register of Historic Places. The 13,000sq ft **Riordan Mansion** (1300 Riordan Ranch St., E of Milton Rd.), 1904 home of timber-baron brothers, features log siding, volcanic stone arches and original Craftsman-style furniture.

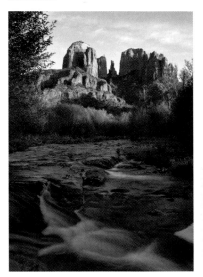

Bed and Board Flagstaff

Lodging
Hotel Monte Vista – *100 N. San Francisco St. / 928-779-1919. $75-$125.* Guest rooms at this four-story remnant of the Roaring Twenties are named after some of the famous folks who once stayed here: Teddy Roosevelt, Humphrey Bogart, Bob Hope and others. Live bands still perform in its lounge, in the heart of Flagstaff's historic district.

Restaurants
Cottage Place – *126 W. Cottage Ave. 928-774-8431. Dinner only. Closed Mon. $30-$50. Continental.* Lodged in a beautiful 1909 bungalow home, this longtime restaurant (since 1980) brings a touch of Europe to Northern Arizona. Diners may start with brie en croute or escargots; then progress to Dijon-crusted salmon, pork schnitzel or a vegetarian asparagus risotto.

From Flagstaff, take US-180 NW to Rte. 64, which leads N to **Grand Canyon National Park★★★**, where the next tour begins.

Tour 2 ➡

Grand Canyon National Park
251 miles   Map following and Atlas pages 18, 44

The Grand Canyon is more than impressive. It is the largest chasm on earth, nearly 2 billion years in the making, 277mi long and averaging 10mi wide and 1mi deep. Hundreds of side canyons, creeks and trails lie within the boundaries of Grand Canyon National Park. No other place has so much of the earth's physical surface and geological history on display.

Practicalities

Visitor Information

Most visitor services are centered on the canyon's South Rim. The main visitor center is located within Grand Canyon Village. Park your car and ride the **free shuttle** or walk a short trail from Mather Point. Free shuttle service is available throughout the Village, and from March to November, along Hermit Road, when Hermit Road is closed to vehicular traffic.

Canyon Floor Trails

The depth of the Grand Canyon—South Rim to canyon floor—is about 5,000ft. The distance on foot, by any of the steep and narrow trails, is 7mi to 10mi. Trailheads may be found at three viewpoints. Most popular is the Bright Angel Trail, originating at Bright Angel Lodge in Grand Canyon Village. The trail descends 4,460ft in 9mi to the Colorado River at Phantom Ranch, which lodges adventurers in cabins or dormitories. The trail is recommended only for exceptionally fit individuals. Signs posted prominently along the canyon rim, and at nearly every trailhead, caution hikers not to try hiking to the river and back to the rim in a single day. An option for descending to the canyon floor is a commercial mule ride: one day down, one day back (reservations should be booked well in advance).

Bed and Board Grand Canyon's South Rim

Lodging

El Tovar Hotel – *Grand Canyon Village. / 303-297-2757. $125-$300.* Native stone and heavy Oregon pine logs create the atmosphere of an old European hunting lodge, and the views are out of this world: El Tovar has offered perspective on the Grand Canyon since 1905. Fresh Atlantic salmon, flown in daily, is a highlight of the **Dining Room** *($30-$50)*.

Maswik Lodge – *Grand Canyon Village. / 303-297-2757. $75-$125.* Motel-style rooms in this modern complex include private bath. In summer,

cabins with double beds and shower are available. Cafeteria, sports bar and gift shop on-site.

Bright Angel Lodge & Cabins – *Grand Canyon Village. / 303-297-2757. $75-$125.* This rustic lodge (1935) is popular with the backpack set. Lodge rooms (some without private bath) are basic but comfortable; most come with one bed. Cabins have private baths. The **Arizona Room** *($15-$30)* serves up ribs, steaks, fish and fowl Southwest style. A family-style restaurant and an ice-cream fountain (summer only) are also on-site.

Begin at the **South Rim**★★★. Most visitor activities in the park are focused along a 35mi strand of

paved road that extends from the East Rim Entrance Station (29mi W of US-89 at Cameron) to Hermits

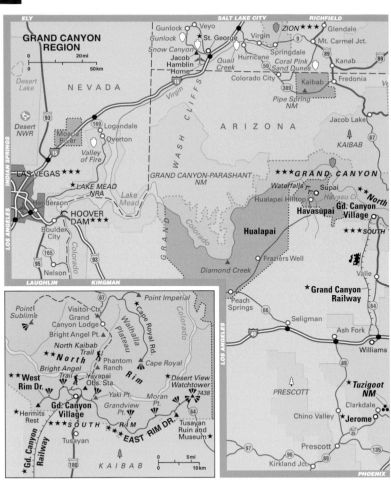

Rest. **Grand Canyon Village** is the site of park headquarters, the main visitor center and the lion's share of historic hotels, restaurants and tourist facilities within the park. This community links East Rim and West Rim drives with Williams (56mi S via Rte. 64) and Flagstaff (80mi SE via US-180). The **Grand Canyon Village Historical District★** comprises nine buildings, including the El Tovar Hotel, Hopi House, Bright Angel Lodge and Lookout Studio. Trains still arrive at the **Santa Fe Railway Station** (1909, Francis Wilson), one of three remaining log depots in the US. The **Buckey O'Neill Cabin** (1890s) was built by a miner-politician who rode with Teddy Roosevelt's Rough Riders in 1898 during the Spanish-American War assault on San Juan Hill.

Perched on the rim west of the Bright Angel Lodge is the **Kolb Brothers Studio** (1904). The two brothers photographed tourists descending by mule into the canyon. The building is now operated as a bookstore and art gallery. A mile east of the visitor center, itself east of the historical district, the **Yavapai Observation Station** contains exhibits on the Grand Canyon's fossil record; guided geology walks depart several times daily. The **Rim Trail** (9.4mi) extends gently west from here to Hermits Rest; its first 2.7mi (to Maricopa Point) are paved and highly accessible.

Take the shuttle (see Practicalities, page 7) along **West Rim Drive★★**, an 8mi road. The drive passes **viewpoints★★★** at Maricopa Point, the John Wesley Powell Memorial, Hopi Point, Mohave Point and Pima Point before ending at **Hermit's Rest★**, built as a tourist stop with a fireplace and picture windows.

Then travel **East Rim Drive★★★** (Rte. 64 E), a 24mi road from

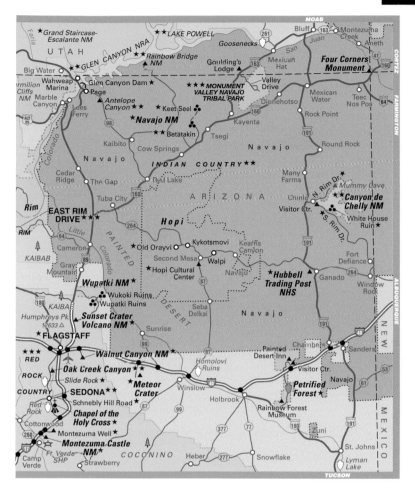

Grand Canyon Village to the East Rim Entrance Station. Viewpoints include Yaki, Grandview, Moran and Lipan Points. A small pueblo

Desert View Watchtower

ruin marks the **Tusayan Ruin and Museum★**, 20mi east of the village. Displays trace the primitive Native American culture of pueblo-dwelling Anasazi in the Grand Canyon region prior to the 13C. The **Desert View Watchtower★**, 22mi from Grand Canyon Village, may be the most photographed structure in the park. Modeled after an ancient Pueblo lookout, the three-story building is dominated by a circular 70ft tower that commands expansive **views★★★** of the convoluted canyon and

Colorado River far below. The Painted Desert appears on the far eastern horizon.

Continue to the junction with US-89 at Cameron and turn right (S). About 15mi south, past Gray Mountain, **Wupatki National Monument★** (Sunset Crater-Wupatki Rd.) holds hundreds of Pueblo-style masonry remains of a farming community that lived here 800 years ago. The highlight of the 55sq-mi preserve is the **Wupatki Ruins**, accessible from an overlook or a .5mi trail. The extraordinary site includes a 100-room pueblo, ball court and amphitheater. The **Wukoki Ruins**, reached by a .2mi trail, consist of an isolated square tower and several rooms, surrounded by the pastel shades of the Painted Desert.

Return S to Flagstaff on US-89, then S to Phoenix via I-17 to end the tour.

Canyonlands of Utah ★★★

Zion NP

The dimension of vast and distorted space is the first thing that strikes visitors to southern Utah's Canyonlands region. The canyons of Zion National Park are surrounded by cliffs as high as 3,000ft. Water only now seeping through the porous sandstone to the canyon floor fell as rain atop these cliffs 1,500 years ago. Bryce Canyon National Park features an astonishing concentration of dizzying, multicolored rock spires and evocatively shaped rocks called hoodoos. Capitol Reef National Park, whose central feature is a 100mi-long rock form known as Waterpocket Fold, is an isolated moon-scape of buttes, mesas and other monoliths that stand 500ft or higher above a level desert floor. Arches National Park is a fantastic landscape of wind- and water-sculpted rocks, formed into improbable swirls, graceful freestanding arches and impressive natural bridges spanning hundreds of feet. Enormous Canyonlands National Park is split into three distinct areas by the confluence of the Colorado and Green Rivers, its colorful rock strata witness to billions of years of geologic history.

St. George is historically important as the earliest Mormon colony in southern Utah. Across the state, Moab, despite its biblical name, might more appropriately be called Mecca, considering its importance to river rafters and mountain bikers as an outdoor-recreation center.

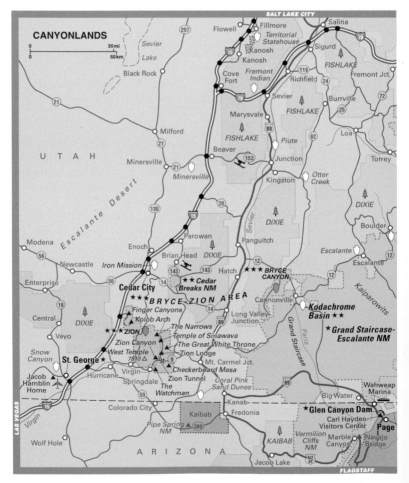

Tour 3

Zion–Bryce Area
405 miles   *Atlas pages 6, 64, 39*

Considered by some to be the most appealing area in all of Utah, this region contains three national parks (Zion, Bryce Canyon and Capitol Reef), two national monuments (Grand Staircase-Escalante and Cedar Breaks), stunning state parks and national forests, accented by an annual dose of Shakespeare in Cedar City. Considerably more developed than the Colorado River canyonlands to the east and south, this area actually has a small metropolitan center. St. George is the largest city in southern Utah; nearby, once-small towns like Hurricane are rapidly transforming into booming desert retirement communities.

Bed and Board Zion–Bryce Area

Lodging

Bryce Canyon National Park Lodge
435-834-5361. Open Apr.-Oct. $75-$125. A shingled roof, stone piers and green shutters reflect the restoration of this 1930s National Historic Landmark to its former rustic elegance. Its porch overlooks the brilliant colors of Bryce's famed hoodoos—tall, red-rock pinnacles.

Desert Pearl Inn – *707 Zion Park Blvd. (Rte. 9), Springdale. / 435-772-8888. $75-$125.* Nestled along the Virgin River at the gateway to Zion Canyon, this lodge is built of fir and redwood from an old railroad trestle. Balconies and terraces give every room a river or cliff view.

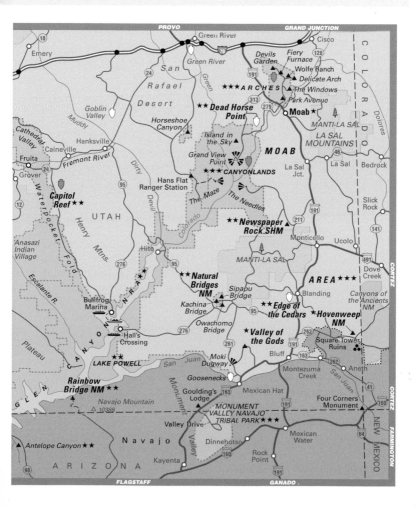

Restaurants

Adriana's – *164 S. 100 West, Cedar City. / 435-865-1234. $15-$30. Continental.* Lodged in a 1916 Victorian manor near the Shakespearean theater, this Olde English eatery offers steaks, chicken and chops served by staff in Renaissance costume. Celtic music accompanies dishes like pork tenderloin with apricot-ginger sauce and grilled rainbow trout.

Cafe Diablo – *599 W. Main St., Torrey. 435-425-3070. $15-$30. Southwestern.* Local trout gets a pumpkin-seed crust, poblano peppers are buried beneath hominy, rattlesnake cakes are topped with rosemary aioli. Everything here has a desert twist: "painted chicken" is coated with honey, lime and tomatillo salsa, and the chipotle-fired ribs heat up diners' tongues.

Begin in **St. George★**, one of Utah's fastest-growing communities, its numbers swelled by throngs of snowbirds and retirees. The **St. George Mormon Temple** (440 S. 300 East), constructed between 1871 and 1877, was the first Mormon temple in Utah. From St. George, drive NE on I-15 to Exit 16 and take Rte. 9 E to Springdale, gateway to **Zion National Park★★★**. Surrounding a scenic, 2,500ft-deep sandstone canyon decorated with waterfalls and damp hanging gardens, Zion is one of the oldest (1919) national parks in the US. More than 65mi of hiking trails lead into its backcountry wilderness. Nonhikers can go on horseback or join shuttle-bus tours of the valley (Apr–Oct). **Zion Canyon**—8mi long, .5mi wide and .5 mi deep—begins at the park's south entrance off Route 9. **Zion Scenic Canyon Drive** runs 8mi to the **Temple of Sinawava**, a natural sandstone amphitheater. (From April to November the road is closed to private vehicles beyond historic **Zion Lodge**, 1mi from Route 9.) From the Temple, a paved 1mi trail follows the Virgin River to **The Narrows**, barely 20ft wide in the river bottom, squeezed between rock walls rising 2,000ft above it. In good weather, wading is permitted; but flash-flood danger is always present. Hikers are advised to check river conditions, posted daily at the visitor center. Continue E on Rte. 9 to Mt. Carmel Junction, turn left onto US-89 and head N to the junction with Rte. 12. Take Rte. 12 SE to

access **Bryce Canyon National Park★★★**. This 56sq mi park contains an array of rock spires, pinnacles, arches and hoodoos tinted in a palette of rich shades, considered by some to be the most brightly colored rocks on earth. Red, yellow and brown shades derive from the iron content in the rocks. Purple and lavender rocks contain more manganese. The odd rocks rise from the floor of a series of vast horseshoe-shaped natural amphitheaters. They reflect the

Bryce Canyon NP

effects of 60 million years of wind and water on the layers of limestone. An 18mi (one-way) scenic drive leads along the pine-clad rim top to popular views and trailheads leading down into the mazelike amphitheaters.

Nine miles south of Cannonville, off Rte. 12, you'll find **Kodachrome Basin State Park★★**. Here, the unique desert terrain features a concentration of tall sandstone chimneys that rise from the desert floor. The spires appear white or gray in midday light. In low-angle sun of early morning or late afternoon, they begin to glow in unexpected shades of crimson, mauve and burnished orange. Hiking and horse-back trails lead to peaceful desert vistas across **Grand Staircase-Escalante National Monument★**, which surrounds the park.

Return to Cannonville and follow Rte. 12 NE through Boulder to Torrey. Take Rte. 24 E 9mi to **Capitol Reef National Park★★**. The visitor center is located at the entrance, near the historic town of **Fruita**. Primarily a backcountry park, it is threaded with miles of unpaved driving roads and hiking trails offering views of vividly colored, 1,000ft-tall cliffs, stone arches and natural bridges. A 10mi one-way scenic drive from the visitor center leads to overlooks of remote canyon country and slick-rock terrain. Unpaved roads such

as the one north from Rte. 24 into **Cathedral Valley**—an area of stunning buttes and freestanding monoliths—are suitable only for high-clearance or four-wheel-drive vehicles.

The park was named by 19C Mormon pioneers, whose travels across Utah were impeded by a huge, eroded rock uplift known as the **Waterpocket Fold**. Stretching 100mi to Lake Powell, it impeded their progress as a coral reef would a ship. This "reef" is crowned by white domed rock that reminded pioneers of the US Capitol building in Washington DC.

Continue on Rte. 24 E along the **Fremont River**, then northeast to I-70. Take I-70 E to Exit 180 and follow US-191 S to Moab to end the tour.

Tour 4

Moab Area
346 miles   *Atlas page 8*

Edging the Colorado River, the small town of Moab serves as gateway to the Arches and Canyonlands National Park areas. Surrounded by breathtaking scenery of carved rock and powerful flowing water, it is the stage for a range of outdoor activities, particularly Colorado River rafting and "slick-rock" mountain biking. Below Moab, the Green River flows into the Colorado, which proceeds through the strong rapids of Cataract Canyon, and empties into Lake Powell before continuing through the Grand Canyon.

Bed and Board *Moab*

Moab Lodging
Sunflower Hill B&B Inn – *185 N. 300 East. / 435-259-2974. $125-$200.* Wooded pathways and flower gardens provide a quiet retreat from nearby downtown Moab. Guests relax on wicker chairs on the covered porch, savor the stone fireplace in the living room or collapse into antique iron beds.

Moab Restaurants
Slick Rock Cafe – *5 N. Main St. 435-259-8004. Under $15. Southwestern.* This hip spot, with petroglyph replicas on walls, is a hangout for mountain bikers and river rafters. Diners munch platters of "Macho Nachos" at tables facing Main Street activity, or dine inside on Utah red trout with herbed cornmeal or a chili verde burrito stuffed with pork, black beans and rice.

Lodging South of Moab
Grist Mill Inn – *64 S. 300 East, Monticello. / 435-587-2597. Under $75.* Built in 1933 as a flour mill, this wooden building has been restored as a B&B. Both the main house and neighboring granary are outfitted with claw-footed tubs, floral patterns and iron beds.

Valley of the Gods B&B – *East of Rte. 261, 9mi north of Mexican Hat. 970-749-1164. Under $75.* This solar- and wind-powered stone ranch house is located in a mini-Monument Valley north of the San Juan River. Visitors enjoy the sights of Red Rock country from the long front porch, or relax in rooms with rock walls and wood stoves.

Begin the tour in **Moab★**, which offers far more lodging and dining options than any other southeastern Utah community. A large number of expedition outfitters and guided-tour operators make their headquarters here.

To access **Arches National Park★★★**, drive 5mi NW on US-191 from Moab to the park entrance, where you'll find the visitor center. The greatest concentration of natural stone arches in the US—more than 2,000—is found in this rugged 120sq mi park. The unique terrain represents the effects of 150 million years of erosion on 5,000 vertical feet of rock, revealing a porous layer of 300ft-thick Entrada Sandstone, out of which today's arches were formed.

Arches NP

Many geological attractions may be seen from the park's 18mi (one-way) main road. Two miles from the visitor center, **Park Avenue** is the name given to a tapering red-rock canyon resembling a city skyline. Seven miles farther, a paved spur road leads 3mi to a clustered group of geological features in **The Windows** section of the park. Short trails reach the major features, which include the North and South Windows, Double Arch and Turret Arch.

Returning to the main road, another spur road (2.5mi farther) leads to the remains of **Wolfe Ranch** and the **Delicate Arch** viewpoint. Delicate Arch is perhaps the park's most recognizable feature. At the end of the main road, the **Devils Garden** area contains numerous arches, including Skyline Arch and Landscape Arch—one of the world's longest, spanning 306ft although it is only 10ft thick in one spot.

Return to US-191, turn right and head NW 6mi to Rte. 313, which heads into **Canyonlands National Park★★★**, to the Island in the Sky District. Utah's largest national park contains 527sq mi of deep, eroded canyons, characterized by sheer cliffs, outstanding mesas and bizarrely shaped hoodoos, balanced rocks, pinnacles and arches typical of southeastern Utah. Trisected by the deep canyons of the Colorado and Green Rivers, Canyonlands' three main sections are reached via different routes, each one far from the other. The rivers are separated by the **Island in the Sky** District (the only section this driving tour visits), a gigantic level mesa. At its tip, 3,000ft above the confluence, is **Grand View Point**, with panoramic views of tiered canyons, in dramatic red, orange and pink layer-cake slices of color in late afternoon or early morning. Below lies the pale White Rim—a rocky sandstone bench—and farther below, the Colorado River (to the east) and Green River (to the west). Return to Moab and follow US-191 S 74mi to Blanding. There, at **Edge of the Cedars State Park★★** (660 W. 400 North), a small museum contains the remains of a pre-Columbian Anasazi Indian village, occupied from AD 700-1200. The ruins include six partially excavated dwellings. There is also a modern museum, which displays a fine collection of artifacts, including pottery and weavings.

South of Blanding, take Rte. 95 W 42mi to **Natural Bridges National Monument★★**, accessible by Rte. 275. This remote parkland contains the eroded stone networks of Armstrong and White Canyons. Over hundreds of centuries, seeping water and seasonal runoff have worn away vast sections of rock walls to create three stunning natural stone bridges that are among the largest in the world. From the visitor center, a 9mi paved park road provides overlooks for viewing **Sipapu Bridge**, the longest and highest; **Kachina Bridge** and **Owachomo Bridge**, the oldest and smallest.

Return E on Rte. 95 about 2mi to the junction of Rte. 261, and take Rte. 261 S to access **Valley of the Gods★**. A four-wheel-drive vehicle is recommended, with plenty of gas for the car and water for its passengers; there are no services whatsoever. Smaller in scale than its southerly neighbor, Monument Valley, Valley of the Gods is far less crowded. Perhaps the best view of Valley of the Gods is from the **Moki Dugway** (Rte. 261), where it descends in 1,000ft of steep switchbacks from Cedar Mesa to the valley floor. A rough 17mi dirt road passes through the valley to reach US-163. Turn right onto US-163 and drive S to reach **Monument Valley Navajo Tribal Park★★★** (Tribal Rd. 42, 4mi east of US-163) in Arizona to end the tour.

Monument Valley's distinctive landscape covers 150sq mi on both sides of the Arizona-Utah border. Massive sandstone monoliths, red in color, rise up to 1,000ft from a relatively flat desert floor. The unpaved 17mi **Valley Drive** (for high-clearance or four-wheel-drive vehicles only) loops through the park and past prominent features, such as The Mittens, Elephant Butte, The Thumb and the Totem Pole. Other monoliths are easily viewed from the visitor center.

Denver and the High Rockies ★★★

Nowhere else in the continental United States are the mountains as high, nor the terrain as challenging, as in the Colorado Rockies. Climaxed by no fewer than 53 peaks of 14,000ft elevation or higher, the Rocky Mountains—actually a series of north-south-running ranges—dominate the western two-thirds of the state of Colorado. Many of North America's most famous ski resorts are found here, along with fascinating pieces of mining and railroad heritage. Denver is closer to high mountains than any other major American city. Yet these very heights keep the city's growth spreading across the plains to its south, east and north. The peaks rise literally from the western suburbs, making state and national parks and forests easy getaways for city dwellers. The Continental Divide winds through this mountainous domain, headspring of three of North America's six longest rivers: the Colorado, Arkansas, and the Rio Grande.

Tour 5 ➤

Downtown Denver
1 mile   *Map following and Atlas pages 10, 40*

Nicknamed the "Mile High City" because its elevation is exactly 5,280ft above sea level, Denver is a rapidly growing metropolis of more than two million people. As the largest urban center between Phoenix and Chicago, Dallas and Seattle—it is the focus of commerce, government, sports and the arts for the greater Rocky Mountain region. The city is nestled near the foothills of the Rockies on a high plain that originally was Arapaho and Cheyenne Indian land. The alpine panorama to its west has become North America's greatest mountain playground, with many famous ski resorts (such as Vail and Aspen) and a remarkable concentration of peaks higher than 13,124ft (4,000m).

Larimer Street

Practicalities

Visitor Information

The Denver Metro Convention & Visitors Bureau at 1555 California St., Suite 300 (303-892-1505, www.denver.org), operates three visitor information centers: Denver International Airport main terminal, Tabor Center (entrance facing Larimer St.) and Cherry Creek Shopping Center. Free information on accommodations, area events and attractions, and dining available.

Shopping

16th Street Mall: 16-block downtown pedestrian mall with national retailers like Ann Taylor, Niketown, and eateries Hard Rock Cafe and others. **South Broadway Antique Row** (1400 S. Broadway): 14 blocks with over 400 dealers in antiques, art and collectibles. **Writer Square** (Lawrence and Larimer Sts., between 15th & 16th Sts.): specialty shops, galleries, restaurants flower market, spa/salon. **Cherry Creek Shopping District** (1st Ave. between Steele St. & University Blvd.): Denver's single most popular visitor attraction is the Cherry Creek Shopping Center (3000 E. 1st Ave.), an elegant indoor mall just north of Cherry Creek Park. The adjacent streets of **Cherry Creek North** (1st to 3rd Aves.) are lined with boutiques, restaurants, galleries, salons and day spas.

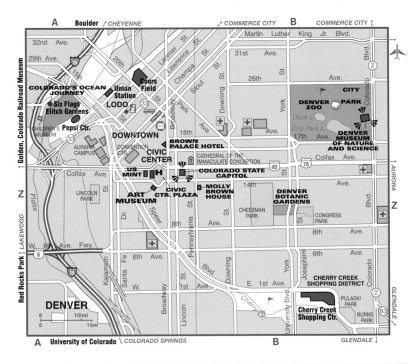

Bed and Board Denver

Lodging

The Brown Palace Hotel – *321 17th St. / 303-297-3111. $200-$300.* When entrepreneurs seeking silver and gold flocked west in 1892, they stayed at this distinguished inn. Presidents still shake hands in the grand atrium, its seven tiers of balconies lined in Mexican onyx and crowned by a stained-glass dome. Celebrities dine at the formal **Palace Arms** *($30-$50)* among European battle flags.

The Oxford Hotel – *1600 17th St. 303-628-5400. $125-$200.* French and English antiques adorn rooms at

Denver's oldest grand hotel. The red-brick exterior is classic; careful restorations have revealed false ceilings and silver chandeliers previously coated in paint. Built in 1891, it is on the National Register of Historic Places.

The Warwick – *1776 Grant St. 303-861-2000. $125-$200.* This elegant midsize hotel has undergone extensive renovation, with data-ports and tasteful new furnishings. An atrium, fitness center, rooftop pool and restaurant add to the first-class image.

Restaurants

The Broker – *821 17th St. 303-292-5065. Dinner only. $30-$50. American.* Partially set in the original vault from a 1903 bank, this city standby is famed for the bowl of steamed, peel-and-eat Gulf shrimp delivered free to every table. The menu features Colorado lamb and filet Wellington, fresh Alaskan salmon and king crab.

Buckhorn Exchange – *1000 Osage St. 303-534-9505. $30-$50. Regional.* Like Theodore Roosevelt and his contemporaries, diners at Denver's oldest restaurant can try elk, pheasant and rattlesnake in the company of more than 500 animal trophies and 125 guns. The eatery uses such indigenous Old West ingredients as chilies and juniper berries.

Restaurant Kevin Taylor – *1106 14th St. / 303-820-2600. Dinner only. Closed Sun. $30-$50. Creative American.* Showcase for the culinary talents of Denver's most acclaimed chef, this Hotel Teatro eatery offers fine dining amid contemporary decor. Chilled terrine of duck foie gras, venison loin over roasted pears, and warm banana parfait make a marvelous meal.

Begin the tour in **Downtown Denver★** at **Larimer Square★★** (1400 block of Larimer St.), a lively, pedestrian-friendly thoroughfare. Larimer Square anchors the southern end of the 26-block historic district. Between Larimer and Wynkoop Sts., 20th St. and Speer Blvd., the **LoDo★★** neighborhood preserves warehouses and other 19C buildings that have been revitalized into restaurants, clubs, galleries, shops and upper-story apartments. Also transformed (1995) was **Coors Field** (2001 Blake St.), a major-league baseball stadium. Take 18th St. SE to Broadway, then S on Broadway to reach the **Civic Center★★** area, dominated by the **Colorado State Capitol★★** (200 E. Colfax Ave.). Constructed in the shape of a Greek cross, the granite capitol is a smaller version of the US Capitol. As the seat of state government, the imposing hilltop capitol building (1886) is home to the General Assembly and offices of the governor and other officials. On the south end of **Civic Center Plaza★**, the **Denver Art Museum★★** (100 W. 14th Ave. Pkwy.) houses exhibits on seven vertically stacked gallery floors. Collection highlights include the **Native American★★★**, **Pre-Columbian and Spanish Colonial★★** and **Western Art★**, the latter showcasing a casting of The Cheyenne, regarded as the best Remington sculpture in existence. Nearby, the **US Mint★★** (W. Colfax Ave. & Cherokee St.), one of four in the country, produces half the coins circulated in the US: it strikes 10 billion coins a year.

Tour 6 ▶

Rocky Mountain National Park–Ski Country
499 miles   *Map following and Atlas pages 9, 10, 40*

Spread across more than 20,000sq mi, yet crossed by only a handful of major highways, Colorado's High Rockies reward visitors with rich flora and fauna, evocative mining heritage, and some of the most spectacular mountain scenery in the country. The driving tour includes a visit to magnificent Rocky Mountain National Park and passage through Colorado's renowned ski country west of Denver.

Rocky Mountain NP

Bed and Board The High Rockies

Lodging

Hotel Jerome – *330 E. Main St., Aspen. / 970-920-1000. Over $300.* Over a century ago, the rich mining crowd bellied up to the cherry-wood bar to celebrate silver strikes. Aspen's elite still frequent the same terra-cotta brick landmark. Glass-cut doorknobs open to Victorian rooms decorated in raspberry and hunter green. Old mining maps and silver-etched lamps line the hallways.

The Lodge at Vail – *174 E. Gore Creek Dr., Vail. / 970-476-5011. Over $300.* Tyrol meets Rockies in an opulent mix 30 yards from Vail's chairlifts. Wide stairs lead to rooms of polished woods, high-backed leather chairs and private balconies. Enjoy Colorado lamb at the **Wildflower Restaurant** *($30-$50)* or pasta in **Cucina Rustica** *($15-$30)*.

The Stanley Hotel – *333 Wonderview Ave., Estes Park. / 970-586-3371. $125-$200.* This white-pillared Georgian hotel served as author Stephen King's setting for *The Shining*. Double fireplaces and staircases still grace the lobby, and Palladian windows provide spectacular views.

Tour Notes: *US-34 (Trail Ridge Road in Rocky Mountain National Park) is closed from Many Park Curves west to the Colorado River Trailhead mid-Oct to Jun due to snow. Rte. 82 south of Leadville to Aspen is closed mid-Oct to Memorial Day due to snow.*

Begin W of **Denver★★★**, in **Golden★★**, former territorial capital of Colorado. Here, the world's largest brewing complex, **Coors Brewing Co.★** (13th and Ford Sts.), offers tours of the beer-making process. Drive W on US-6 along Clear Creek to Rte. 119, heading N on the **Peak to Peak Highway★★** (Rtes. 119, 72 & 7), a scenic route that winds through pine woods offering occasional mountain views. In **Nederland★**, an erstwhile mining-supply town, proceed N on Rte. 72. After 14mi, look for a left turn to **Brainard Lake★**, surrounded by the snow-cloaked summits of the Indian Peaks Wilderness on the Continental Divide. Continue N on Rte. 72, then follow Rte. 7 N to the town of **Estes Park★★**, a tourist town of shops, inns, restaurants and nearly 5,500 residents.

Take US-36 to enter **Rocky Mountain National Park★★★**. This magnificent landscape boasts craggy mountains, glaciated valleys, perpetual snowfields, small lakes and vast alpine tundra that covers one-third of its 415sq mi. It

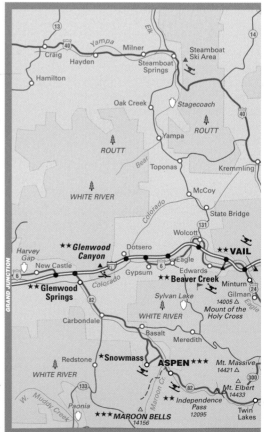

Restaurants

Renaissance – *304 E. Hopkins St., Aspen. / 970-925-2402. Dinner only. Closed mid-Apr–mid-Jun & Oct–late Nov. Over $50. French.* To this restaurant's chef-owner, a great meal is like a great painting in which attention has been paid to even the finest brush stroke. An example is crusted Chilean sea bass with artichokes, shiitake mushrooms and foie gras. Nearby at 216 S. Monarch St., **Rustique Bistro** (*$15-$30*) offers a less-pricey alternative with such fare as duck cassoulet and braised short ribs.

Sweet Basil – *193 E. Gore Creek Dr., Vail. / 970-476-0125. $30-$50. Contemporary American.* The menu features more than 100 mountains

changes seasonally, but this contemporary bistro always remains packed from wall to mustard-colored wall. Unique dishes include halibut with black-truffle risotto, seared duck with mango spring rolls, and saffron linguini with lobster. The main-floor wine bar is a popular local gathering place.

The Hearthstone – *130 S. Ridge St., Breckenridge. / 970-453-1148. $15-$30. Regional.* A late-19C Victorian home one block off Main Avenue is the setting for this friendly restaurant. Upper-story windows offer views of nearby mountains. Generous portions of wild game, steaks and seafood are the fare, complemented by an award-winning wine list.

of 11,000ft or higher, reaching its apex at 14,255ft Longs Peak, dominating the park's southeast corner. The **Beaver Meadows Visitor Center** has park maps and information on ranger-led tours and lectures. From here, 10mi **Bear Lake Road**★ runs south,

providing access to trailheads. Return to US-36 and travel NW to join US-34, bearing left (W) onto US-34. The highest continuous paved highway in North America, 48mi **Trail Ridge Road**★★★ (US-34, from Estes Park to Grand Lake) ascends rapidly from coniferous and aspen forests to treeless tundra

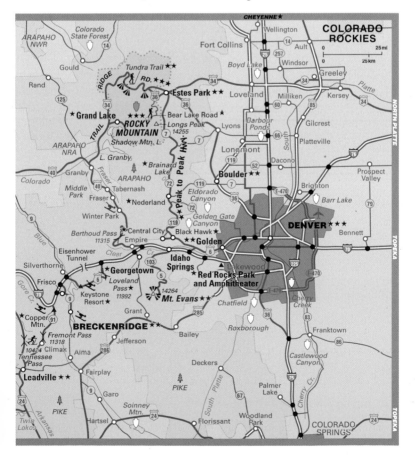

at 12,183ft, offering outstanding mountain panoramas. Viewing areas include **Many Parks Curve**★★ and **Forest Canyon Overlook**★★. After passing its high point, the road curves downhill past the **Gore Range Overlook**★ and the **Alpine Visitor Center** (closed in winter), crossing the Continental Divide at 10,758ft Milner Pass.

Continue S on US-34 to **Grand Lake**★, a small town of Old West-style log buildings and boardwalks at the west entrance to the park. Proceed S to Granby, turn left onto US-40 and follow it S 46mi to I-70 at Empire. Head W on I-70 to begin the driving tour of Colorado's ski country.

The old town center of **Georgetown**★ (Exit 228 from I-70) is immaculately preserved. Built in 1875 by a French immigrant, the **Hotel de Paris**★ (409 6th St.) is now a museum. The 1879 **Hamill House**★ (305 Argentine St.) demonstrates the luxury in which the family of a silver baron lived. Tickets for a 1hr summer round-trip outing on the **Georgetown Loop Railroad**★★ (1106 Rose St.) are available at the historic train depot.

Continue 23mi W on I-70 through the **Eisenhower Tunnel**, bored under the Continental Divide at 10,700ft. North America's highest road tunnel enables vehicles to avoid 11,992ft **Loveland Pass**★— a scenic but time-consuming 20mi traverse. The highway passes ski areas **Arapahoe Basin**, **Keystone Resort**★ and **Breckenridge**★★ (Rte. 9). Now a resort town, Breckenridge was founded in 1859 by gold miners. Its Main Street is lined with restaurants and shops, most housed in colorfully painted Old West-style buildings. **Country Boy Mine**★ (542 French Gulch Rd.) offers tours and gold panning in French Creek.

Continue W on I-70 to Exit 195. Exiting the interstate at charming **Copper Mountain Resort**★, Rte. 91 cuts across 11,318ft Fremont Pass before descending into **Leadville**★★, once Colorado's

silver capital. Today its wide main street is still flanked by fine Victorian architecture, and the side streets are lined with brightly painted dwellings, from mansions to modest miners' cottages. Nearby, the **National Mining Hall of Fame and Museum**★★ (120 W. 9th St.) has exhibits on historic and contemporary mining, including a full-size, walk-through replica of a hard-rock mine.

From Leadville, travel S on US-24 to Rte. 82, the Independence Pass Highway, which links US-24 with I-70 at Glenwood Springs. Rte. 82 crosses 12,095ft **Independence Pass**★★ and offers incredible views from numerous hairpin turns. Snow normally closes the 38mi stretch from Twin Lakes (6mi west of US-24) to Aspen from mid-October to Memorial Day

Follow Rte. 82 W to **Aspen**★★★, a town synonymous with glamour. Its ski terrain ranks among the finest in North America. High-season guests and part-time residents include many celebrities. Known for chic boutiques and fashionable restaurants, historic downtown focuses on a three-block pedestrian mall. The **Aspen Music Festival and School**★★★ (2 Music School Rd.) presents summer concerts that often feature world-renowned musicians. Rising directly behind town, Aspen's original ski mountain lures some of the world's best skiers—but no snowboarders. The **Silver Queen Gondola**★★ operates in summer for sightseeing; views from its summit take in four surrounding wilderness areas.

Optional detour: Some 13mi southwest of Aspen rise Colorado's most oft-photographed mountains, the **Maroon Bells**★★★. The view of these massifs is particularly inspiring across **Maroon Lake**★★. Summers and weekends, private vehicles are prohibited from 10mi Maroon Creek Road, so shuttle buses make the trip from Rubey Park Transit Center (Durant Ave. between S. Galena & S. Mill Sts.). In winter, the **T-Lazy-7 Ranch** (Maroon Creek Rd.) operates snow-mobile tours and sleigh rides.

From Aspen, travel NW to I-70, passing **Glenwood Springs**★★ with its **Hot Springs Pool**★★ (401 N. River St.)—claimed to be the world's largest naturally spring-fed hot pool. Drive E on I-70 along **Glenwood Canyon**★★ and the Colorado River to Vail.

One of North America's premier mountain resorts, **Vail**★★ is tightly packed into the Gore Creek valley. Vail Village retains pedestrian-only streets and chalet-style buildings with fashionable shops and restaurants. Satellite developments that extend from East Vail to West Vail include Lionshead and Cascade Villages. All sit at the foot of mammoth **Vail Mountain**★★★, the continent's largest single-mountain ski area—with 32 lifts, over 4,600 acres of terrain, and a 3,360ft vertical drop. The **Colorado Ski Museum**★ (231 S. Frontage Rd.) documents the state's skiing and snowboarding heritage. Established by the former First Lady, the tranquil **Betty Ford Alpine Garden**★★ (173 Gore Creek Dr.) maintains 1,500 varieties of annuals and perennials, with a special focus on high-elevation plants. **Adventure Ridge**★ is the site of outdoor ice-skating, snow tubing, night ski-biking and high-mountain snowmobile and snowshoe tours.

Continue E on I-70 to Exit 240 and the old mining town of **Idaho Springs**, where 19C commercial buildings housing restaurants and bars, gift shops and Western wear, line the main street. The 1913 **Argo Gold Mine & Mill** (2350 Riverside Dr.) is an ore-processing mill open for self-guided tours, with a small mining museum and an opportunity to pan for gold. At the **Phoenix Gold Mine**★ (right on Stanley Rd., left on Trail Creek Rd.), a retired miner leads an underground tour.

Return to Golden via Rte. 119 and US-6 to end the tour.

San Juan Country ★★

Colorado's southwestern corner is a largely mountainous area dominated by the sharply angled slopes and precipices of the San Juan Mountains. The Rockies' youngest range includes more than 2 million acres of national forests, parks and designated wilderness areas laced with scenic rivers and lakes. Fourteen lofty peaks surpass 14,000ft; at lower elevations, agriculture still holds sway.

Historic 19C mining towns characterize human settlement in the high San Juans. But long before white settlement, the Anasazi were present. Between AD 600 and 1300, they built primitive cities amid the piñon-and-sage mesas feathering off the San Juans. Abandoned seven centuries ago, these communities are now some of the best preserved archaeological sites in the Southwest. The foremost cliff-dwelling sites in the world are contained within Mesa Verde National Park.

Mesa Verde NP

Bed and Board San Juan Country

Lodging

Strater Hotel – *699 Main Ave., Durango. / 970-247-4431. $125-$200.* The Strater is a palace of red brick and white trim with a hint of the Wild West, furnished with a fabulous collection of Victorian walnut antiques, embellished with brass rails and brocaded settees. Rooms boast four-poster beds and ornate wallpaper.

New Sheridan Hotel – *231 W. Colorado Ave., Telluride. / 970-728-5024. $125-$200.* A century ago, the New Sheridan would indeed have been "new." Today the fully restored inn is a classic of Victorian elegance, its rooms adorned with period furniture and photos of early Telluride. A historic bar and the gourmet **Chop House** (*$30-$50*) restaurant lure locals.

Tour 7 ▶

Durango–Telluride–Mesa Verde National Park
308 miles   Atlas pages 8, 9

Begin the tour in the Animas River town of **Durango★**, founded in 1880 when the Denver and Rio Grande Railroad built a rail line to alpine mines near remote Silverton. Be sure to ride the **Durango & Silverton Narrow Gauge Railroad★★★** (479 Main Ave.), which still employs coal-fired steam locomotive engines to pull restored narrow-gauge cars 45 slow miles through San Juan National Forest. The train depot anchors the **Main Avenue National Historic District★** (Main Ave., 5th-12th Sts.). The star attraction here is the **Strater Hotel★** (699 Main Ave.), a four-story brick Victorian that first let rooms in 1887. It contains a hiss-the-villain summer theater and the Diamond Belle Saloon, a bar with a honky-tonk pianist and garter-clad waitresses. From Durango, drive N 50mi on US-550 to **Silverton★** (at Rte. 110), an 1880s boom town with 50-or-so Victorian buildings in the historic district (10th, 15th, Mineral & Snowden Sts.). Continue N 25mi on US-550, which cores through country pocked by abandoned mines along the **Million Dollar Highway★**. Just before Ouray, stop to see the impressive **Box Canyon Falls**. Once in **Ouray★**, take time to enjoy the seven-block **Main Street Historic District** and the **Ouray Hot Springs Pool** (north end of town), with its million gallons of thermal water.
Drive N 10mi from Ouray on US-

550; at Ridgway, turn left (W) onto Rte. 62. After 23mi, turn left (E) on Rte. 145 and continue 17mi to **Telluride★★**. This mountain resort town consists of a Victorian **National Historic District** nestled in a steep-sided glacial box canyon, linked to an ultra-modern **Mountain Village** by a state-of-the-art gondola and a 6mi road. The acclaimed **Telluride Ski Resort★★** is one of the Rockies' most challenging: its 3,522ft vertical drop is accessible from the historic district or Mountain Village. In summer, Telluride is noted for its diverse festivals— bluegrass, jazz and chamber music, film and hang-gliding.
Drive S 65mi from Telluride on Rte. 145 to the small town of **Dolores**. While here, be sure to see the historic train station and the rare **Galloping Goose** (Rte. 145), a hybrid train/bus contraption that once simultaneously carried passengers and removed snow from the railroad tracks. Detour W 3mi on Rte. 184 to the **Anasazi Heritage Center★**, a museum displaying native artifacts removed from a valley before it was flooded by a reservoir. Continue S 12mi from Dolores on Rte. 145 to the agricultural town of **Cortez**, which features an eight-block historic district along Main Street.
Take US-160 E 10mi from Cortez and turn S into **Mesa Verde National Park★★★**, which preserves mesa-top structures and cliff

dwellings displaying construction methods used by ancestral Puebloans between AD 750 and 1300. The 21mi drive from the park entrance to **Chapin Mesa Archaeological Museum**★ offers magnificent **views** of four states. Adjacent to the museum, **Spruce Tree House**★★★ is a major cliff dwelling. Nearby is 6mi **Mesa Top Loop Road** (open year-round); overlooks provide views of **Square Tower House**★★, the **Twin Trees**★ site and **Sun Temple**★. In warmer weather, guided tours are offered to spectacular sites built into overhanging cliffs at **Cliff Palace**★★ and **Balcony House**★★.

Return N to US-160, and continue E 36mi to Durango to end the tour.

Santa Fe Area ★★★

Known as the "Land of Enchantment," northern New Mexico is a cultural mélange of ancient and modern Indian and Spanish, American pioneer and high-technology influences. Stark adobe architecture contrasts to strikingly blue skies, tower-ing mountains and precipi-tous gorges. Though not its largest city, the state capital of Santa Fe is considered New Mexico's cultural and tourism hub. Santa Fe is an hour's drive north of modern Albuquerque and an hour's drive south of the rustic mountain art town of Taos.

Bed and Board Albuquerque

Lodging
The Hotel Blue – 717 Central Ave. NW. / 575-924-2400. $75-$125. An Art Deco-style "chic boutique" hotel wedged between downtown and Old Town on Route 66, the Blue brings a Route 66 sensibility into the 21C. Rooms are simple, but display modern frills. **Corvette's Diner** (under $15) is reminiscent of a 1950s soda fountain.

La Posada de Albuquerque – 125 2nd St. NW. / 575-242-9090. $75-$125. The only historic hotel in Albuquerque has a two-story lobby of arches and balconies centered on a tiled fountain. New Mexico's tallest building when Conrad Hilton opened it in 1939 on the site of a livery stable, it has been fully restored. Each room boasts Spanish tile and hand-carved furnishings; **Conrad's Downtown** ($15-$30) serves three meals daily.

Restaurants
The Artichoke Cafe – 424 Central Ave. SE. / 575-243-0200. $15-$30. Mediterranean-American. A charming bistro in a historic neighborhood east of downtown, this bright, artsy corner draws lunchtime diners with its sandwiches, salads and pasta entrées. Dinner may begin with a steamed artichoke (with three dipping sauces); main courses include pan-seared duck breast (with pomegranate glaze) and daily seafood specials.

Maria Teresa – 618 Rio Grande Blvd. NW. / 575-242-3900. $15-$30. New Mexican. A classy restaurant in an 1840 hacienda near Old Town, Maria Teresa is an Albuquerque institution. The menu features continental dishes along with regional specialties. Many diners blend the two, beginning with a bowl of tasty tortilla soup and continuing with one of the signature steak dishes.

66 Diner – 1405 Central Ave. NE. 575-247-1421. Under $15. American. A tribute to the days when Route 66 was the "Mother Road," this white, Art Deco-style diner serves all the meals you'd expect, from blue-plate specials to cheeseburgers with fries and a Coke. Service comes with a bubble-gum smile.

Tour 8

Albuquerque–Santa Fe–Taos
267 miles

Atlas pages 21, 22, 38, 62

Begin the tour in New Mexico's largest city, **Albuquerque★**, an intriguing mix of old and new, of 14C Indian pueblos, 18C Spanish village and 21C high-technology. Its architecture is liberally sprinkled with reminders of its mid-20C fling as a prime stop on cross-country Route 66, in the days before the interstate highway system. Pueblo Revival architecture, neon-lit cafes and motor courts speckle its cultural corridors, especially Central Avenue east and west of downtown.

In **Old Town★★**, some 150 shops and galleries face hidden gardens and cobbled walkways around a tree-shaded 18C plaza. The **Church of San Felipe de Neri★** (1706; reconstructed 1793) has been in continuous use. Pueblo and Navajo artisans display wares at the small Indian market along San Felipe St. Highlights of the Old

San Felipe de Neri

Town area are the **Albuquerque Museum of Art and History★★** (2000 Mountain Rd. NW), with its extensive collection of Spanish Colonial artifacts and works by New Mexico artists; the **New Mexico Museum of Natural History and Science★★** (1801 Mountain Rd. NW, 4 blocks north and east of Old Town plaza); and the **National Atomic Museum★★** (1905 Mountain Rd.), where exhibits trace the development of atomic energy and weaponry.

A mile from Old Town, the place to get an overview of cultures as presented by the Native Americans themselves is the **Indian Pueblo Cultural Center★★** (2401 12th St. NW, 1 block north of I-40).

Here, the arts of New Mexico's 19 Pueblo communities are exhibited. On weekends, traditional dancers perform on an outdoor stage, and artisans demonstrate various crafts. Four miles west of Old Town (3mi N of I-40), **Petroglyph National Monument★★** (4735 Unser Blvd.

"Ghost Town"

NW), preserves more than 20,000 petroglyphs dating from AD 1300-1650. The carvings—human, animal and ceremonial forms—are accessed by hiking trails.

From Albuquerque, drive E on I-40 to Exit 175 and head N on Rte. 14, the **Turquoise Trail★★**. This 52mi back road runs along the scenic eastern edge of the Sandia Mountains. The route passes dry washes and arroyos and visits a series of revived "ghost towns"— artsy villages suitably weather-beaten but colorfully painted— before opening into a broad, arid plain south of Santa Fe. At **Cedar Crest** (4mi north of I-40), the **Museum of Archaeology and Material Culture** (Rte. 14) has a fine collection on early Native Americans, including Sandia Man, one of North America's earliest fossil-man discoveries.

Rte. 14 leads north into **Santa Fe★★★**, a world-renowned center for the arts, cuisine and shopping at the foothills of the Sangre de Cristo Mountains (7,000ft elevation). This former Spanish capital, founded in 1609, is home to outstanding museums, restaurants and summer opera. Santa Fe's closely monitored adobe architecture nestles around a historic **Plaza★★**, surrounded with art galleries and shops that wind down **Canyon Road★**.

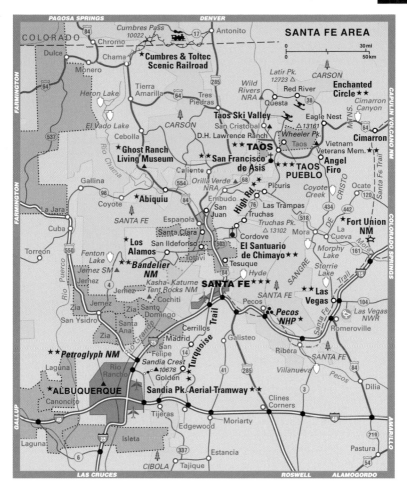

Bed and Board *Santa Fe*

Lodging

Inn of the Anasazi – *113 Washington Ave.* / *575-988-3030. $200-$300.* With traditional beamed ceilings of peeled log, sculpted stairways and intricately patterned pillows, the inn's design is a rich blend of Southwestern cultures. Indian baskets and cacti adorn a lobby with a warm fireplace. The **Anasazi Restaurant** *($30-$50)* focuses on regional cuisine, including coriander-crusted venison.

Hotel Santa Fe – *1501 Paseo de Peralta.* / *575-982-1200. $125-$200.* The only Native American-owned hotel in Santa Fe is characterized by Puebloan artwork and a traditional terrace design. The three-story building features dance performances and storytellers who immerse guests in Picuris culture. The **Corn Dance Café** *($15-$30)* focuses on indigenous cuisine: bison tenderloin, quail with quinoa.

Las Palomas – *119 Park Ave. 575-988-4455. $125-$200.* Guests at these casitas also are welcomed at the nearby Eldorado Hotel, a large resort with such amenities as a rooftop pool. But Las Palomas' rambling courtyards, trickling fountains and gardens are much more intimate. Odd-sized door-ways and uneven walls add genuine adobe charm, and breakfast is delivered to each room in a basket.

El Rey Inn – *1862 Cerrillos Rd. 575-982-1931. $75-$125.* Best of the Cerrillos Road motels south of the Plaza, El Rey ("the King") succeeds with its Spanish Colonial architecture and tended grounds. Built in the 1930s, renovated and well maintained, the motel boasts a Southwestern decor of hand-painted tiles and hand-crafted furnishings.

Restaurants

Coyote Cafe – *132 W. Water St. 575-983-1615. Over $50. Creative Southwestern.* Most agree the original Coyote Cafe is worth the hype. In the kitchen where dishes like duck-confit tacos and chipotle-grilled quail were first concocted, black-truffle risotto brings a smile to vegetarians' faces. At the sunny **Rooftop Cantina** ($15-$30), prickly-pear margaritas are the drink of choice.

Geronimo – *724 Canyon Rd. 575-982-1500. $30-$50. Creative American.* Southwest tradition and 21C innovation merge in this old adobe (1748). In this sophisticated space, savor chef-prepared entrées like sautéed quail breast with polenta, sea scallops with caviar citrus sauce or elk medallions with native mushrooms and foie gras.

El Farol – *808 Canyon Rd. 575-983-9912. $15-$30. Spanish.* At this popular Canyon Road outpost, plates of tapas give way to live music—blues, salsa, flamenco—as twilight fades to dark. From puerco asada (pork with figs) to boquerones (marinated white anchovies), El Farol ("the Lantern") serves authentic Iberian "little plates."

Maria's New Mexican Kitchen – *555 W. Cordova Rd. / 575-983-7929. $15-$30. New Mexican.* Strolling mariachi troubadours serenade diners as cooks craft handmade tortillas on an open grill. Servers carry platters of burritos, tacos and blue-corn enchiladas with Spanish rice. A Santa Fe institution of 50 years, Maria's offers more than 100 varieties of margaritas.

On the north side of the Plaza, the **Palace of the Governors**★★ (105 W. Palace Ave.) was the original seat of power for Spanish, Mexican and, later, Anglo governors. Built in 1610, the low, flat-roofed hacienda is one of the oldest occupied buildings in the US, and has been a museum since 1909. Exhibits depict Santa Fe history, from Spanish Colonial through the Anglo frontier era to today.

One block east of Plaza, the **Cathedral Church of St. Francis of Assisi**★★ was intended to resemble great cathedrals of Europe. Unlike other local churches, it is not built in adobe style.

Three blocks northwest of the Plaza, the **Georgia O'Keeffe Museum**★★ (217 Johnson St.) holds the largest collection of paintings, pastels, watercolors and sculptures by the famed artist. O'Keeffe was fascinated by the textures created by light and color in the landscape of New Mexico, her adopted home from 1949 until her death.

Southeast of the Plaza, the **Museum of Indian Arts and Culture**★★ (710 Camino Lejo) highlights the cultural history of New Mexico's Pueblo, Navajo and Apache tribes, and the **Museum of International Folk Art**★★ (706 Camino Lejo) showcases the largest folk collection in the world. From Santa Fe, head north on US-84/285. Along this route, you can visit three of the **Eight Northern Indian Pueblos**, well known for their traditional, handmade arts and crafts (the public is generally welcome to view special feast days, including traditional Indian dances).

Tesuque Pueblo (7-10mi north of Santa Fe) has adobe structures dating from AD 1250. A popular flea market is held adjacent to the hilltop amphitheatre of **The Santa Fe Opera**★★.

Pojoaque Pueblo (12mi north of Santa Fe) is the site of the new **Poeh Cultural Center and Museum**, the nearby Pojoaque (po-WAH-kay) Pueblo Visitor Information Center, with a shop offering crafts by 800 Native American artisans, and the Cities of Gold casino-hotel.

Nambe Pueblo (1mi east of Rte. 503), inhabited since 1300, is known for its stone sculptures, black-and-red micaceous pottery, textiles and beadwork. Several ancient ruins may be found near the Nambe Falls Lake and Recreation Area.

At Santa Cruz, turn right onto Rte. 76, the **High Road to Taos**★★, which runs east 25mi to Rte. 518 near Vadito. Traditional 19C lifestyles persist in a string of villages along this mountainous route, beginning in the weaving center of Chimayo. Here the Spanish adobe church **El Santuario de Chimayo**★★ is the most important pilgrimage site in the Southwest. Some 30,000 pilgrims walk here every Good Friday from as far away as Albuquerque. In the wood-carving village of **Cordova**, crafts are often sold from roadside stalls. The farming hamlet of **Truchas** sits atop a mesa beneath snow-capped

El Santuario de Chimayo

13,102ft Truchas Peak. In the village of **Las Trampas** is the San José de Gracia Church, an oft-photographed Spanish Colonial adobe structure. East of Vadito, take Rte. 518 N to Rte. 68 north into the Spanish colonial town of Taos.

Bed and Board *Taos*

Lodging
Fechin Inn – *227 Paseo del Pueblo Norte. / 505-751-1000. $125-$200.* This inn pays tribute to Russian-born Nikolai Fechin's lithographs, prints and whimsical wood carvings. Window frames, mantels and beams recall the sunbursts and vines of the artist's own home on the self-contained six-acre estate. Many rooms have kiva fireplaces and patios.

The Historic Taos Inn – *125 Paseo del Pueblo Norte. / 505-758-2233. $75-$125.* Beginning in 1895, Taos County's first physician rented small adobes in this complex to artists and writers. Rooms showcase kiva fireplaces and bedspreads loomed by Indian weavers. **Doc Martin's** *($15-$30)* serves plates of tamales, blue-corn enchiladas and piñon-encrusted salmon.

Restaurants
Manou – *4167 Rte. 68, Ranchos de Taos. / 505-751-1684. Dinner only. Closed Tues. $30-$50.* Contemporary American. Housed in a 150-year-old adobe near San Francisco de Asis Church, this restaurant offers carefully prepared dishes that blend creativity with tradition. Start with the spinach and toasted goat cheese salad and move on to a main course of braised Colorado lamb, duck leg confit or grilled Angus ribeye.

Orlando's – *1114 Don Juan Valdez Ln. at Paseo del Pueblo Norte. 505-751-1450. $15-$30. New Mexican.* Cozy, casual and festive, especially on the crowded patio, Orlando's has won Taoseños' hearts with its chile-smothered enchiladas and burritos, carne adovado and fish tacos.

Taos Pueblo

The rustic, Spanish colonial town of **Taos**★★ is perhaps 300 years old. Built around a cozy plaza that remains the heart of the modern town, Taos is today a center for the arts, much smaller than Santa Fe but equally alluring to aficionados of Southwest art. One block east of Taos Plaza, **Kit Carson Home and Museum**★★ (E. Kit Carson Rd.) illustrates Carson's career and frontier life of that era; displays include guns, saddles and period equipment used by mountain men and Indians. Carson, a famous

San Francisco de Asis

frontier scout and Indian agent, lived in this house from 1843 until his death.

The top attraction in town is **Taos Pueblo**★★★, 2mi north of Taos Plaza via Camino del Pueblo. The oldest and best-known New Mexico pueblo has been designated a World Heritage Site by the United Nations. A visit is a step back in time. Although Pueblo Indian ruins are found throughout the Southwest, here the site is intact, occupied and used daily. South of the plaza (4mi via Rte. 68), **San Francisco de Asis Church**★★ is probably the most painted and photographed church in all New Mexico. Georgia O'Keeffe and Ansel Adams immortalized the stark form of this heavily buttressed adobe structure, built between 1710 and 1755. From Taos, head N on US-64 to the junction of Rte. 522. This route is part of the **Enchanted Circle**★★ Scenic Byway (Rtes. 522 & 38 and US-64) north and east of Taos. The 85mi Scenic Byway circles 13,161ft Wheeler Peak, New Mexico's highest point, and connects Taos with several small resort towns. Travel N to **Questa**, starting point for white-water trips on the Rio Grande. Turn onto Rte. 38, heading E to the old mining town of **Eagle Nest**. There, detour 23mi E on US-64 to **Cimarron**, once a stop on the mountain branch of the Santa Fe Trail. Between 1865 and 1880, Wyatt Earp, Billy the Kid and other famous Western characters passed through Cimarron. Back at Eagle Nest, travel SW on US-64, detouring on Rte. 434 S to tiny Angel Fire, a year-round resort. Return to Taos on US-64 W to end the tour.

Road to Enchanted Circle

Big Bend Area ★★

Located in Texas' westernmost corner, El Paso is separated from the Lone Star State's other population centers by more than 500mi of high desert. It's even in a different time zone than other Texas cities. Geography is dominated by the Rio Grande, the great river that sculpts the international boundary between Texas and Mexico. The most dramatic scenery is found 300mi southeast of El Paso in the canyons of isolated Big Bend National Park. Much of the wilderness there belongs to wild animals like mountain lions and javelinas.

Bed and Board Big Bend Area

Lodging

Hilton Camino Real – *101 S. El Paso St., El Paso. / 915-534-3000. $125-$200.* At 17 stories, this historic landmark overlooks three states in two nations. Decked in brass, cherry and marble, the lobby is topped by a Tiffany glass dome of mosaic leaves and blue sky. The ambience of **The Dome** restaurant takes fine dining back to the turn of the 20C.

Lajitas Resort – *Rte. 170, Terlingua. 915-424-3471. $125-$200.* Remote and historic, this 1915 cavalry post once protected the Big Bend area from Mexican bandits. Now it's a full Old West experience—with modern recreational additions like a golf course. Lodgings include the Badlands Hotel and Officer's Quarters, with planked facades and covered wooden sidewalks, on the dusty main drag.

Gage Hotel – *102 US-90 West, Marathon. / 915-386-4434. $125-$200.* This adobe-style inn, built in 1927, is an ideal place to pause en route to Big Bend. Some rooms have fireplaces; all boast historic artifacts. **Café Cenizo** (*$15-$30*), entered off a rustic patio, features mesquite-smoked codorniz (quail stuffed with wild rice) and shrimp tossed with slivers of jalapeño.

Gardner Hotel – *311 E. Franklin Ave., El Paso. / 915-532-3661. Under $75.* This three-story brick hotel is neat, tidy and the region's best bargain. Rooms have original antique furniture, with cable TV and new phones added. Located just a mile from the Mexican border, the Gardner includes the 10-dorm-room El Paso International Hostel (*under $75*).

Restaurants

La Posta de Griggs – *9007 E. Montana Ave., El Paso. / 915-598-3451. $15-$30. New Mexican.* The Griggs family has passed its recipes between generations for more than a century. Today, in a rustic antique ambience, their cozy inn still draws throngs for the rolled tacos, tamales and chili con carne.

Los Bandidos de Carlos and Mickey *1310 Magruder St., El Paso. 915-778-3323. $15-$30. Mexican.* With cathedral ceilings and terra-cotta tiles, this tribute to the Revolution is the city's prettiest Mexican restaurant. Hacienda walls have photos of everyone from Pancho Villa to Miss Texas. The menu features green chile stew and tacos in adobe sauce.

Starlight Theatre – *Rte. 170, Terlingua. / 915-371-2326. Dinner only. $15-$30. American.* This 1940s Adobe Deco theater has been given a new life as a dinner theater where live music and stage shows accompany satisfying meals. Diners might start with wild boar sausage on mixed field greens, then enjoy a chicken breast sautéed with mushrooms and spinach in a cream sauce.

Tour 9 ▸

El Paso–Big Bend National Park
581 miles

Atlas pages 33–37

Begin in **El Paso★**, the largest US-Mexico border city after metropolitan San Diego. The **El Paso Museum of Art★★** (Santa Fe and Main Sts.) is the vanguard of downtown revitalization in the 14-block

Union Plaza cultural and entertainment district. The museum's broad collections include works by Cézanne, Picasso, Frederic Remington and Van Dyck, as well as pieces created in the American Southwest and Mexico since 1945. Four miles southeast of downtown, **Mission Trail**★ (I-10 Zaragoza Exit) links 17C missions that once lured settlers as farming and ranching centers. Northernmost is **Mission Ysleta** (Zaragoza Ave. at S. Old Pueblo Dr.), completed in 1692. Floods destroyed the original mission; this one dates from 1851 and it is still used for religious services. The **Tigua Indian Cultural Center**★ (305 Ya Ya Lane) has a museum, restaurant, gallery and weekend dances. **Mission Socorro**★ (Socorro Rd., 2.6mi south of Mission Ysleta) was rebuilt after a 19C flood. An outstanding example of Spanish Mission architecture, with hand-sculpted roof beams, the mission is the oldest continuously active parish in the US. Also still in use, the gilded **Chapel San Elceario**★ (Socorro Rd. in San Elizario, 6mi south of Mission Socorro) is noted for its late adobe architectural style. It combines Southwestern attributes with European features such as buttresses.

From El Paso head S via I-10, then E to Kent. Take Rte. 118 S to Alpine, passing **McDonald Observatory**★, one of the world's top astronomy research centers (telescope tours available). At Rtes. 17 and 118, **Fort Davis National Historic Site**★★ (Main St., in Fort Davis), built in 1854, is one of the best surviving examples of a frontier post.

Follow Rte. 118 S 103mi through Alpine to Study Butte, the west entrance to **Big Bend National Park**★★★. Located where the Rio Grande takes a sharp turn from southeast to northeast, Big Bend spans 1,252sq mi of spectacular canyons, bottomlands, desert and woodlands. Cut deep into the Chisos Mountains, the limestone chasms and the surrounding Chihuahuan Desert are rich with animal, bird and plant life. Big Bend has more species of migratory and resident birds than any other national park. Bats, rodents and other small mammals are nocturnal; javelina and deer are often seen, mountain lions rarely. Reptiles thrive in the extreme climate. Park headquarters and the main visitor center are at **Panther Junction** (US-385 and Rio Grande Village Rd.) in the heart of Big Bend. Visitor centers at **Persimmon Gap** (US-385 at north entrance), **Chisos Basin** (Basin Rd.) and **Rio Grande Village** (Rio Grande Village Rd.) provide information on archaeology and ecotourism. From Panther Junction, take US-385 N 69mi to Marathon. Turn E on US-90 for 115mi to Langtry, site of the **Judge Roy Bean Visitor Center**★. The story of the Wild West's most famous frontier judge is told in dioramas and exhibits.

Big Bend National Park

Continue E on US-90 for 18mi to **Seminole Canyon State Park**★★, with its 4,000-year-old pictographs. Continue E on US-90 for 27mi to reach **Amistad National Recreation Area**★, popular for water sports. Much of 85mi-long Lake Amistad is lined with limestone canyons, some containing caves with prehistoric pictographs.

Continue on US-90 and take that route to conclude the tour in Del Rio.

Las Vegas ★★★

Las Vegas is the largest and most distinctive resort destination in the world—a 20C boomtown based on gambling, entertainment and recreation. Known for its spectacular casinos, lavish hotels, world-class entertainment and garish bad taste, Las Vegas is without peer or counterpart on the planet.

Bed and Board Las Vegas

Lodging

Four Seasons Hotel Las Vegas – *3960 Las Vegas Blvd. S. 702-632-5000. $200-$300.* Occupying the 35th to 39th floors of the Mandalay Bay Resort's glass tower is this quiet, elegant retreat. The non-gaming hotel combines spacious rooms with top-end shops and an intimate spa. Every element is sublime, from poolside misting devices to filet mignon with tiger prawns in the **Charlie Palmer Steak** *($30-$50)* restaurant.

Bellagio – *3600 Las Vegas Blvd. S. 702-693-7111. Over $150.* Arguably Vegas' most sophisticated casino-hotel, this property offers Northern Italian sensibility in its decor and ambience. Fountains in an eight-acre lake, Chihuly glass sculpture in the lobby, a fine-art museum and botanical conservatory, fine restaurants, and a strict no-unaccompanied-minors policy all add to its adult appeal.

The Venetian – *3355 Las Vegas Blvd. S. / 702-414-1000. Over $150.* The Strip's first all-suite hotel boasts huge standard rooms (700sq ft), a spa run by the renowned Canyon Ranch, the new Guggenheim Hermitage Museum with masterworks from two of the world's great art collections, and a replica of Venice's Grand Canal, lined with shops and fine restaurants.

Restaurants

Aureole – *at the Mandalay Bay. 702-632-7401. Over $50. American.* This high-tech restaurant boasts a four-story, glass-enclosed wine tower with 10,000 bottles. The top-shelf menu includes citrus-braised lobsters and fruit-wood-grilled salmon with sage ratatouille and fennel.

Le Cirque – *at Bellagio. 702-693-7223. Over $50. French.* With real monkeys climbing the walls, life is a circus at Le Cirque. The colorful decor doesn't detract from the serious food. The signature dish is braised rabbit in Riesling with morel mushrooms; leg of lamb is rolled in garlic, rosemary and thyme.

Olio! – *at the MGM Grand. 702-891-7775. Over $50. Italian.* Eclectic, imaginative and ultra-hip, Olio! has everything from fire-sand pits to a private broadcast studio in its lounge. The antipasto and dessert buffets are extravagant, and blue-potato gnocchi and polenta upside-down cake are delectable.

Delmonico Steak House – *at The Venetian. / 702-414-3737. $30-$50. Creole-American.* Not a typical steakhouse, this spacious restaurant is an updated take on Chef Emeril Lagasse's New Orleans eatery. Diners may relax in the piano bar after chateaubriand for two, a double-cut pork chop or blackened snapper. Lagasse also has a seafood cafe in the MGM Grand *(702-891-7374, $30-$50).*

Piero's Restaurant – *355 Convention Center Dr. / 702-369-2305. $30-$50. Italian.* Locals love this celebrity magnet, an old-time Vegas place with tiger-print carpeting and a lively bar. Stone-crab claws and mixed-grill items are served at booths lining the walls.

Tour 10 ➤

Downtown and The Strip
5 miles

Atlas page 47

This tour begins in the older section of Las Vegas and travels north to south along The Strip to reach the newer casino-hotels. A selection of these casino-hotels is described as attractions only; ratings reflect degree of tourism interest, not lodging recommendation.

Begin downtown at the **Fremont Street Experience**★★ on Fremont St. between Main St. & Las Vegas Blvd. Suspended 90ft over downtown, this illuminated extravaganza of flashing, rolling images was designed to rejuvenate tourism along five blocks that have been a principal thoroughfare since 1905. Until the 1960s, Fremont Street was the focus of Vegas' gaming industry. Patrons were enticed to clubs and casinos like **Fitzgeralds**, the **Golden Nugget** and **Benny Binion's Horseshoe Club**. A 60ft-tall talking cowboy, **Vegas Vic**★★, has been an icon since 1951.

From Fremont, turn right onto Las Vegas Blvd. to drive **The Strip**★★★, a 4.5mi stretch (2000-4000 blocks) extending from the Stratosphere in the north to Mandalay Bay Resort in the south. The Strip embraces Las Vegas' greatest concentration of resorts and casinos. Or, take the **Strip Trolley**, which makes stops at major Strip casinos and a detour to the Las Vegas Convention Center.

Stratosphere★ – This 1,149ft tower is capped by a 12-story "pod." Four double-deck elevators climb from the ground-floor casino to the **observation deck** in 30 seconds; **views**★★ are tremendous. The **High Roller** (coaster) loops around the outside of the pod, while riders of the Big Shot ascend 160ft up the building's mast before free-falling with a force four times gravity.

Circus Circus★ – Famed for the live trapeze artists and tightrope walkers beneath the "Big Top" of its main casino, this casino entertains younger guests with roller coasters, water rides, a bungee-cord trampoline and laser tag in the five-acre **Adventuredome**, America's largest indoor theme park.

Treasure Island at the Mirage★★ – In keeping with a buccaneer theme, a well-orchestrated **battle show**★★ between a pirate ship and a British man-o'-war blasts away periodically in a "Caribbean lagoon" outside the entrance. **Mystère**★, a Cirque de Soleil fantasy, plays twice nightly within.

The Mirage★★ – South Seas flair is bolstered by a tropical "island" with lagoons, waterfalls and a **volcano**★★ that spews fire, smoke and burning coconut-scented oil. Behind the hotel are dolphin pools and a zoo enclosure. **The Secret Garden of Siegfried & Roy**★ houses white tigers and other exotic animals appearing in a nightly magic show.

The Venetian★★★ – An engaging imitation of Venice, Italy, the resort features architectural replicas of the **Doge's Palace**, **St. Mark's Square**, the **Campanile** and **Rialto Bridge**. Singing gondoliers pole vessels along the replicated **Grand Canal**★★, lined by a faux-15C street of shops and restaurants. The **Guggenheim Hermitage Museum** is just off the lobby; **Madame Tussaud's**★ portrays in wax 100-plus celebrities from sports, film and entertainment.

Imperial Palace Hotel & Casino – The **Antique & Classic Auto Collection**★ displays 200 of a collection of 750 cars, motorcycles and trucks—among them Elvis Presley's 1976 Cadillac Eldorado, and several Model J Duesenbergs.

Caesars Palace★★ – Imperial Rome sets the theme for this vast complex, adorned with majestic fountains and marble statues, including a copy of Michelangelo's

Caesars Palace

David. The **Forum Shops**★★, a sumptuous mall in the form of a Roman street, have a skylike ceiling illuminated to simulate passing days and nights.

Bellagio★★★ – A lake with twice-hourly **light and fountain shows**★★ graces the foreground of this opulent complex, designed to recall a village on Italy's Lake Como. From a conservatory, visitors enter the **Bellagio Gallery of Fine Art**★★, where rotating exhibits may feature Fabergé eggs or works by Rembrandt, Van Gogh and Picasso. Famed for its restaurants, the resort will not admit minors who are not hotel guests.

Paris Las Vegas★★ – Towering over scaled-down likenesses of the **Arc de Triomphe**, the Champs-Elysées and a Parisian marketplace is a 50-story replica of the **Eiffel Tower**★★, sporting an observation deck reached by glass elevators. The casino is set amid old Paris streets complete with cobblestones and street lamps.

Aladdin★ – From out of 1,001 Arabian Nights comes this exotic resort, built on the site of its imploded namesake—where Elvis and Priscilla Presley married in 1967. Its central feature is **Desert Passage**★, which re-creates fabled North African outposts. Within the hotel is the **London Club**, Vegas' first private European-style casino.

New York-New York★★ – This building simulates the Manhattan skyline with 12 skyscrapers, including a 47-story version of the **Empire State Building**. The street-level facade is a tableaux of other structures, such as a 150ft-tall **Statue of Liberty**★★. Inside, the casino is in a pastiche of Central Park. The **Manhattan Express** roller coaster dips through the roof in a 144ft plunge at 67mph.

MGM Grand★ – With over 5,000 guest rooms, one of the world's largest hotels reflects a Hollywood theme in its shops and decor. **CBS Television City**★ features a studio walk with screening rooms for TV pilots. **Lion Habitat**★, where visitors may get close to a half-dozen live cats, extends the theme of the 45ft bronze lion (on a 25ft pedestal) at the hotel entrance.

Excalibur★ – This complex suggests a castle bristling with ramparts, battlements and bailey towers, from which an automated Merlin wages magical battle against a mechanical dragon. Keeping with the Camelot theme, the hotel shopping mall is a Medieval village with wandering minstrels.

Luxor★★ – A 10-story **sphinx** stands before this stunning 36-story **pyramid**. By night a 315,000-watt laser—the **Xenon Light**★★—shoots from the pyramid's apex into the sky. On an

New York-New York

atrium terrace is the **Tomb and Museum of King Tutankhamen**★, a copy of the original Egyptian tomb and its artifacts.

Mandalay Bay Resort & Casino★ – A tropical water theme lends elegance to a resort noted not only for its restaurants, theater and events center, but also for an artificial wave pool and beach. In the **Shark Reef**★★ aquarium, 100 sharks, crocodiles, moray eels and venomous lionfish glide through a replicated sunken temple.

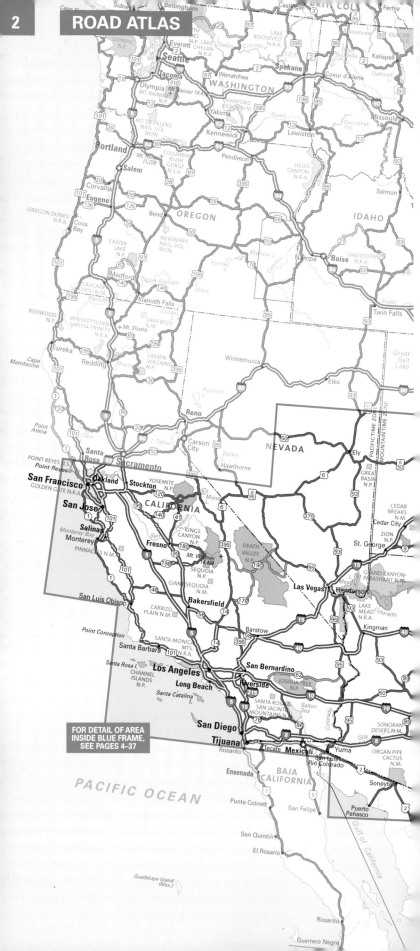

FOR DETAIL OF AREA
INSIDE BLUE FRAME,
SEE PAGES 4–37

PACIFIC OCEAN

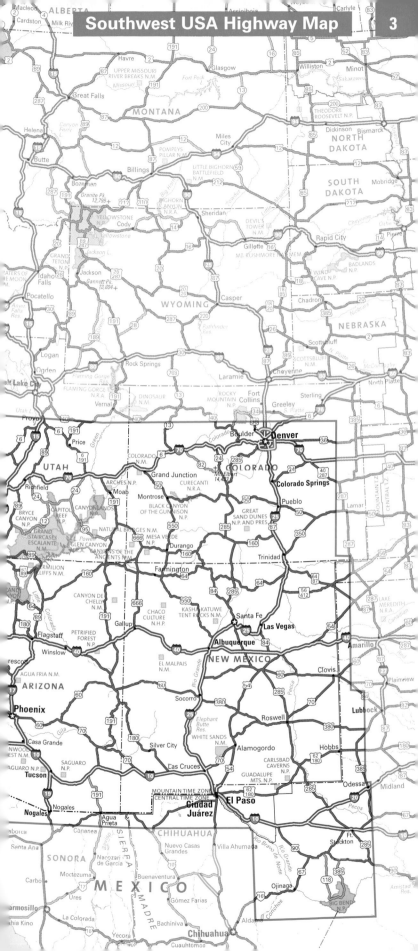

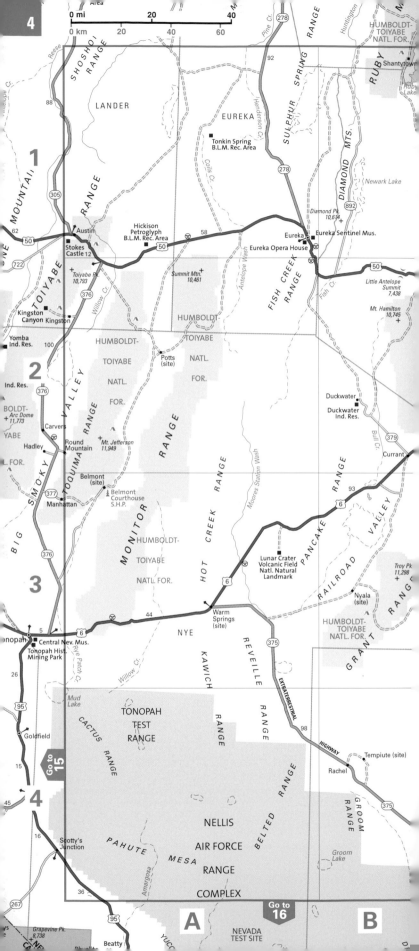

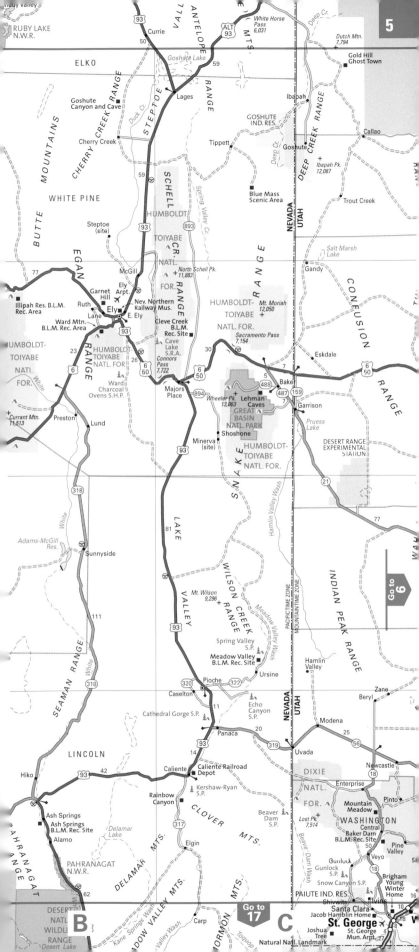

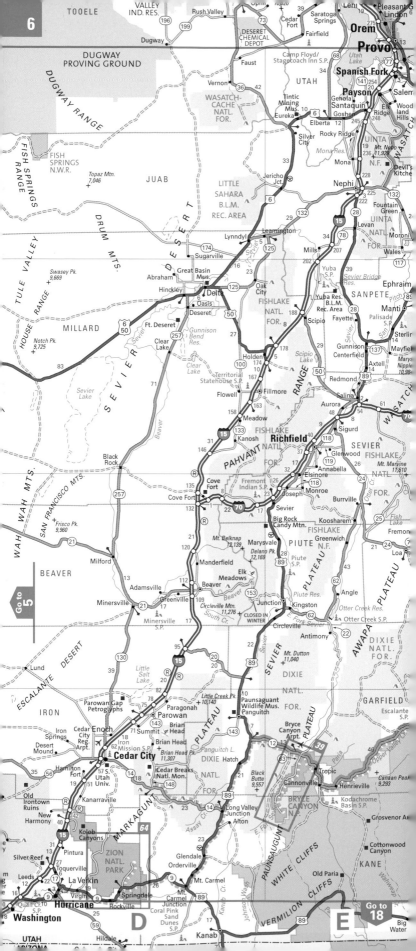

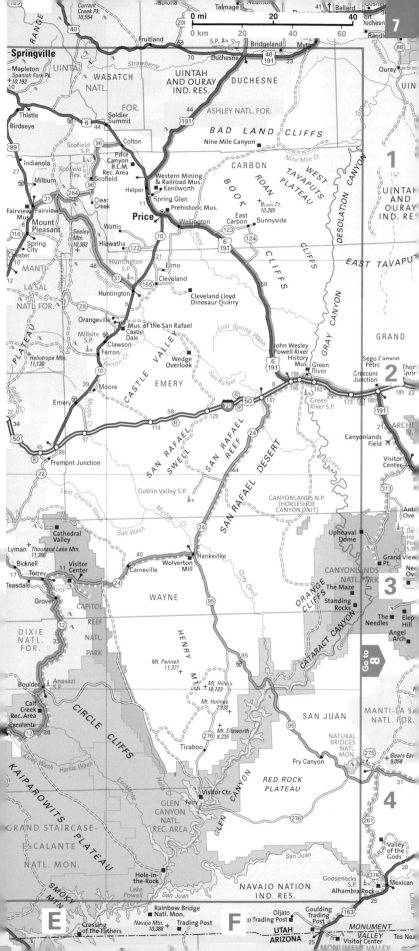

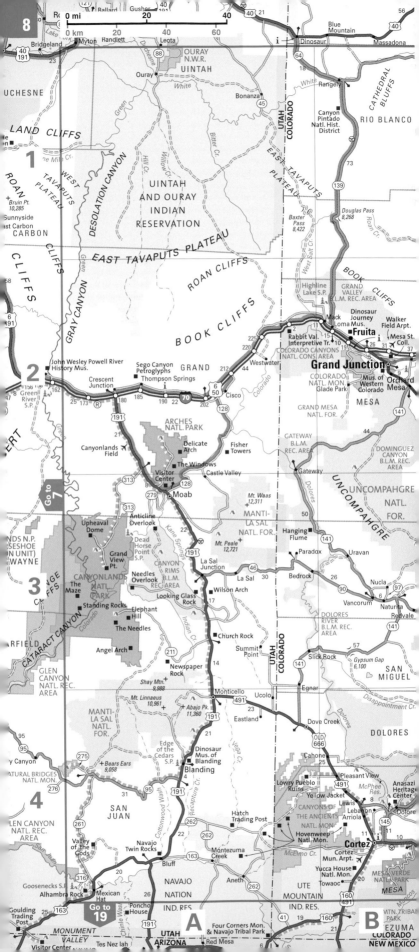

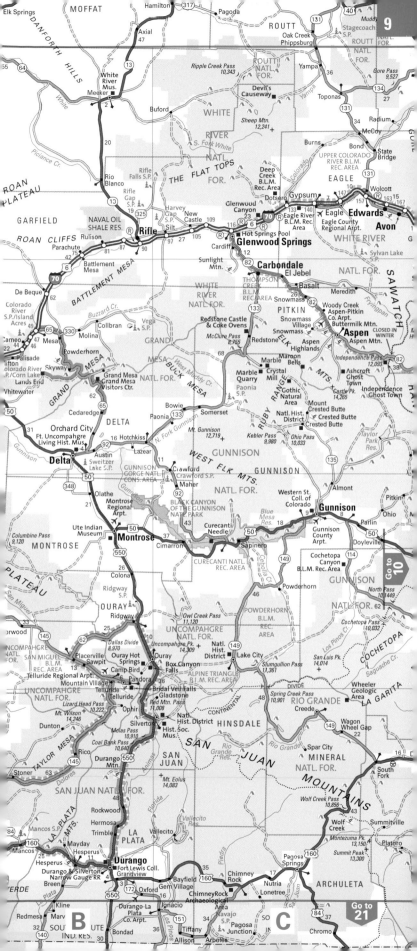

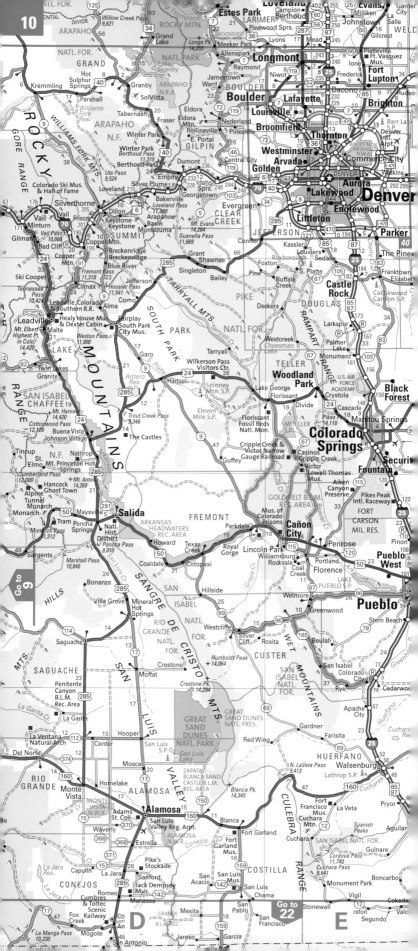

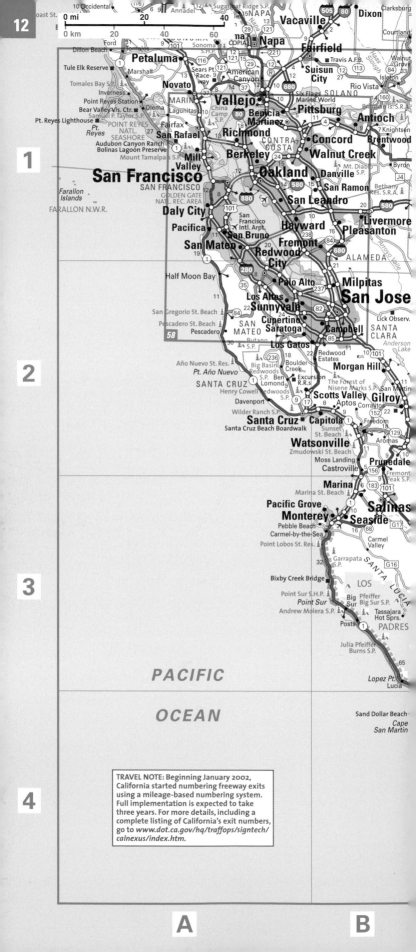

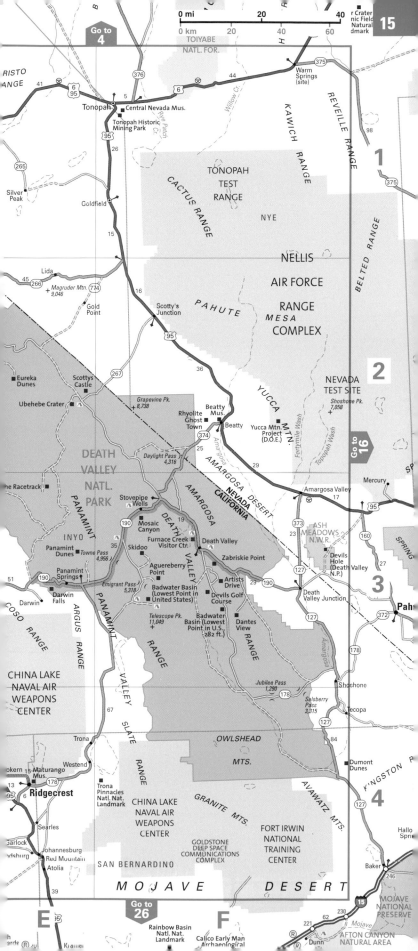

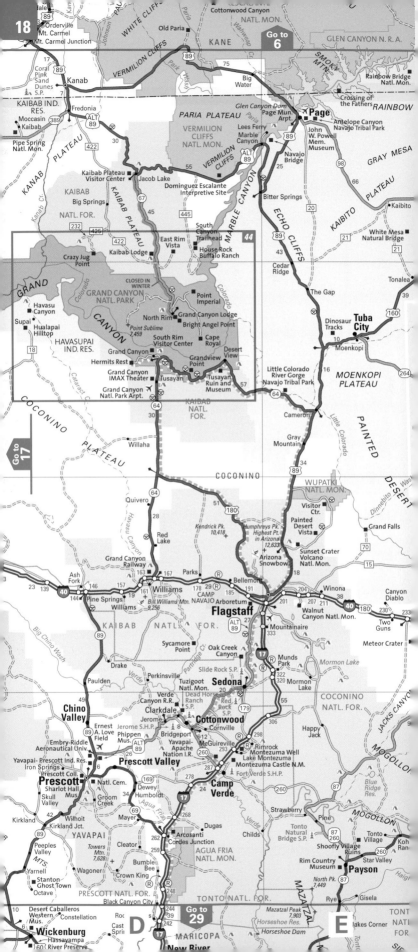

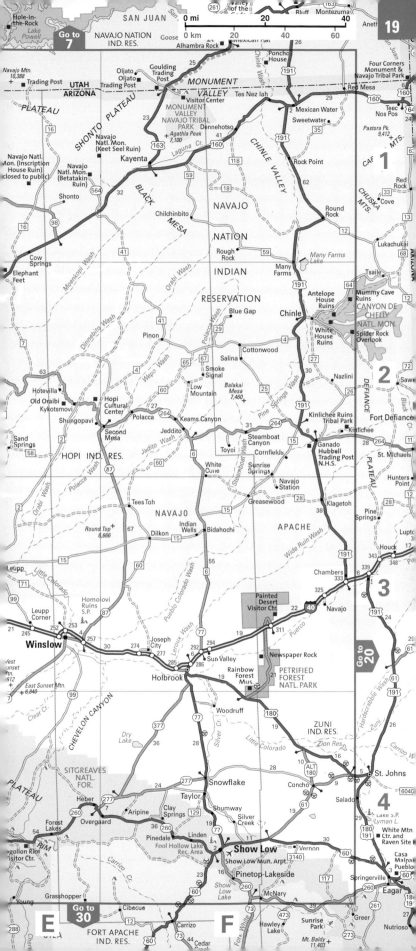

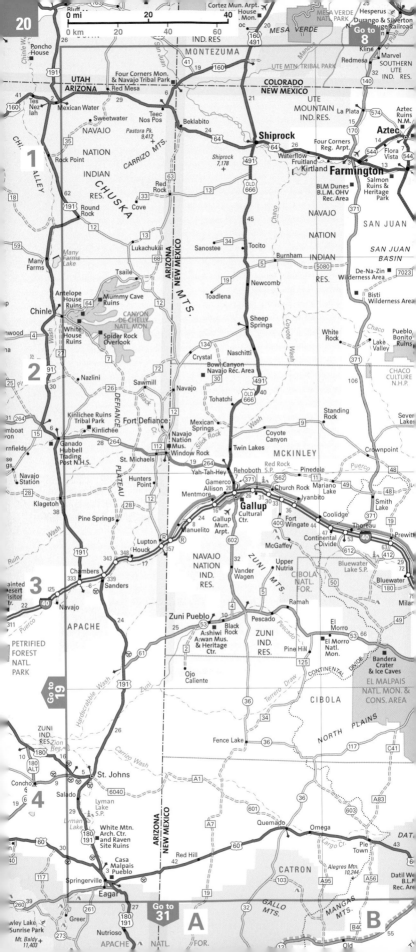

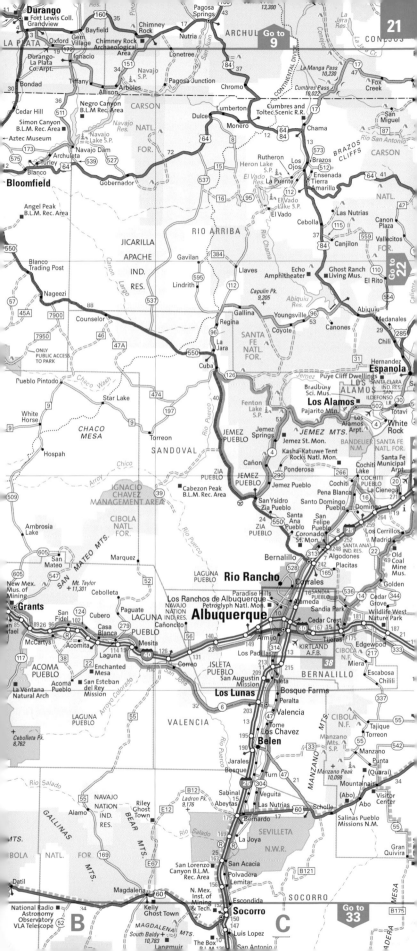

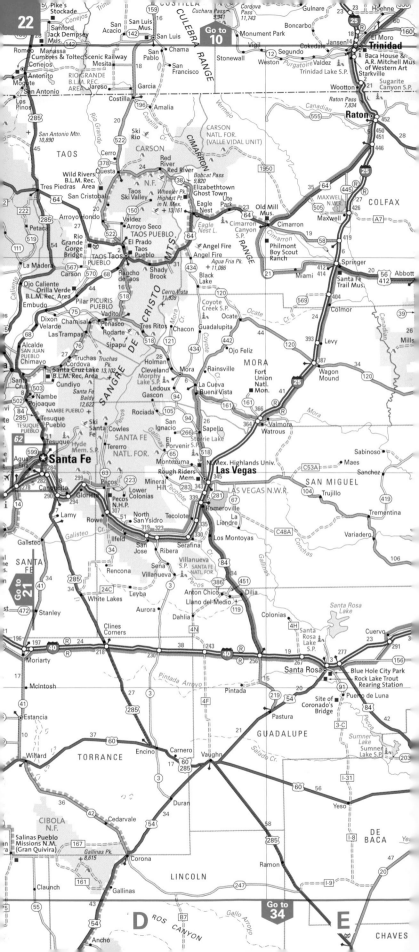

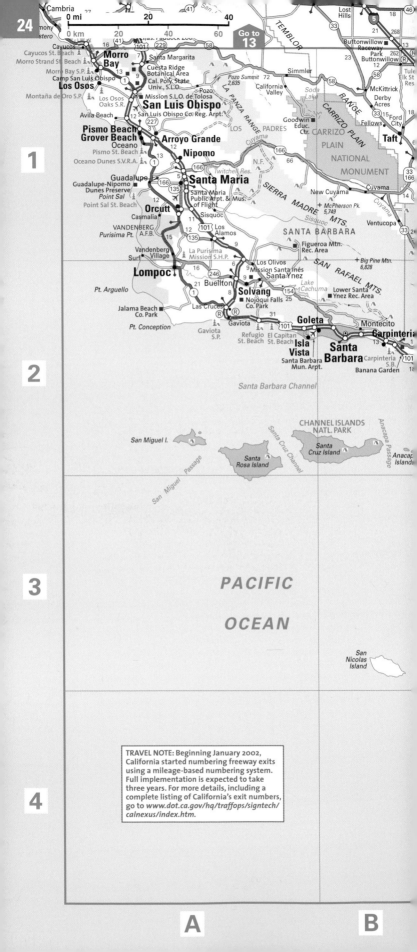

TRAVEL NOTE: Beginning January 2002, California started numbering freeway exits using a mileage-based numbering system. Full implementation is expected to take three years. For more details, including a complete listing of California's exit numbers, go to *www.dot.ca.gov/hq/traffops/signtech/calnexus/index.htm.*

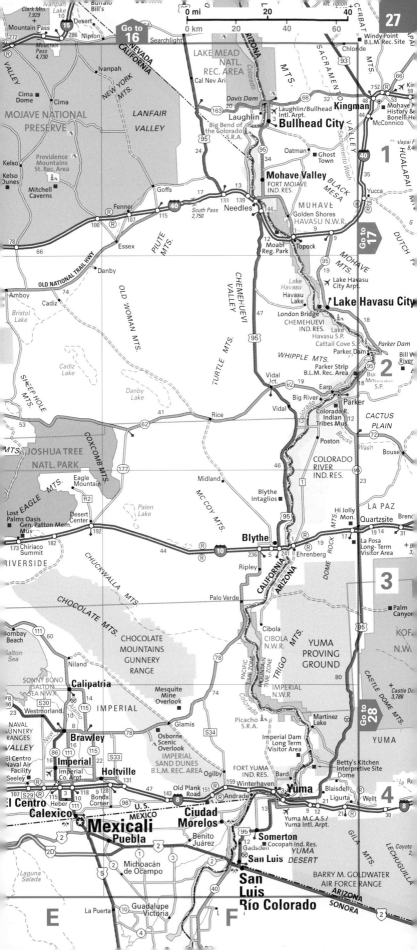

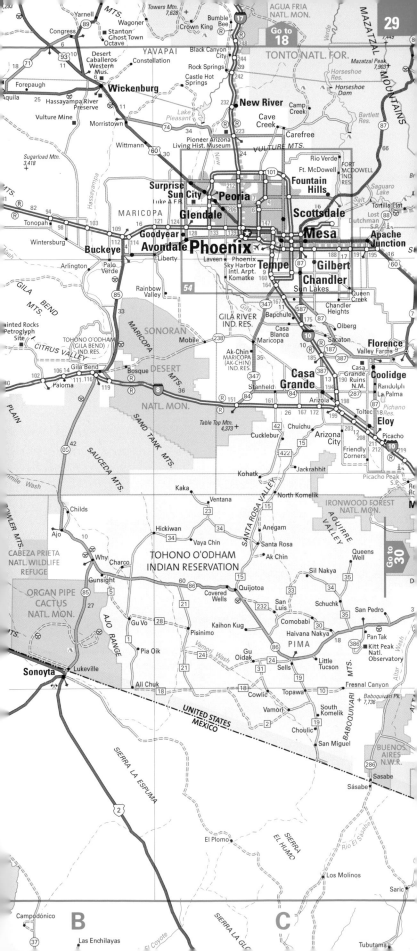

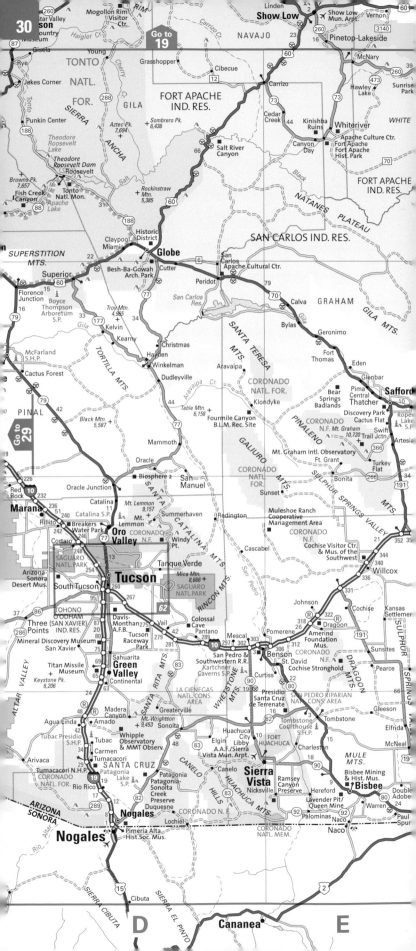

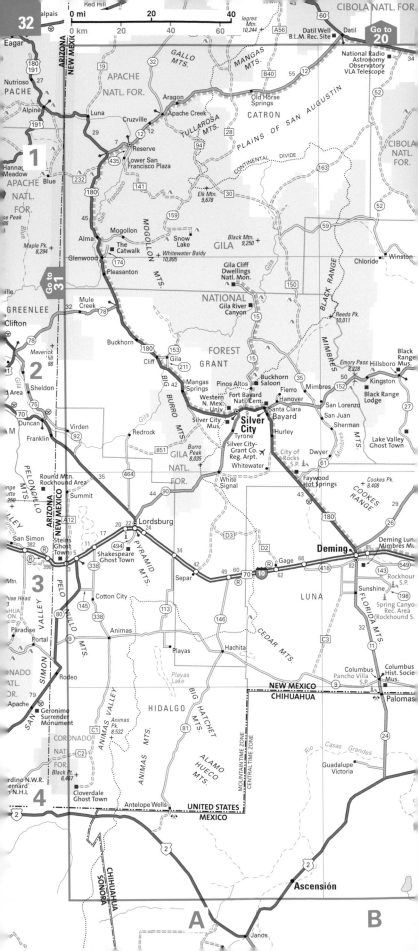

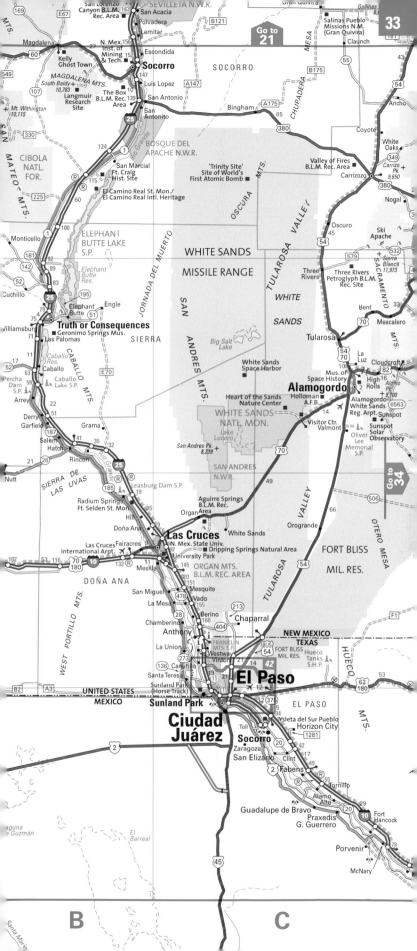

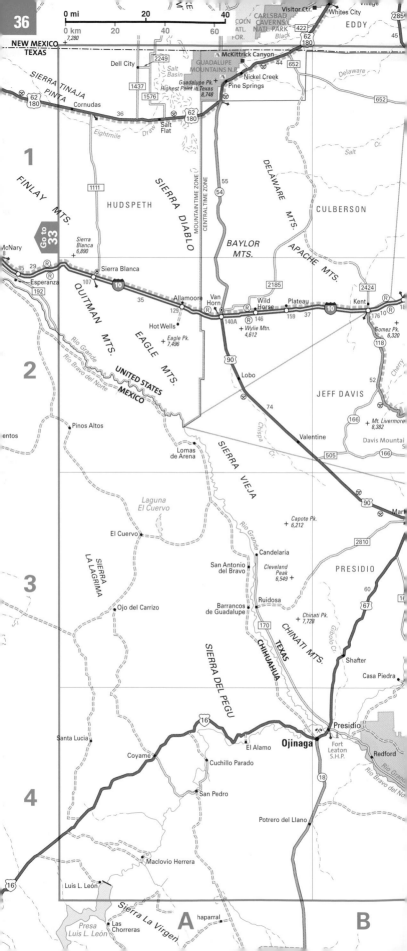

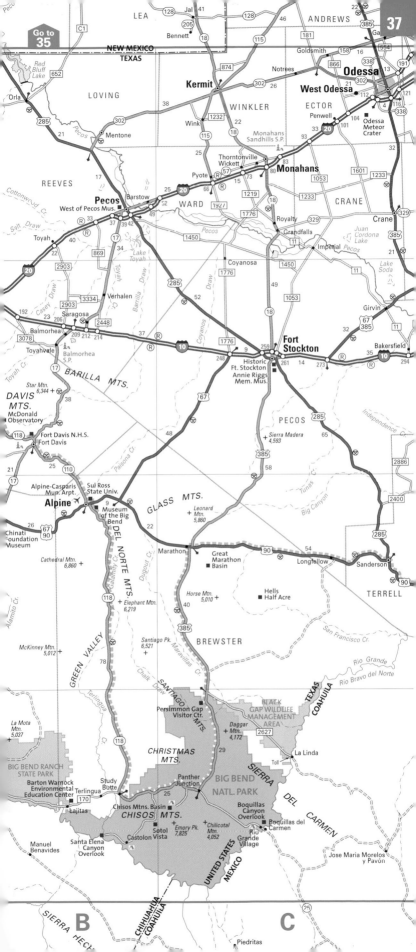

38 **Abeytas–Arriba**

Figures after entries indicate population, page number, and grid reference.

CITY AND PARK MAPS

INDEX

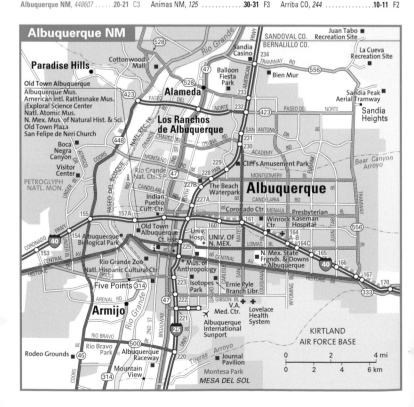

Albuquerque NM

Entries in **bold black** indicate counties.
Entries in **bold color** indicate cities with detailed inset maps.

Arriola–California Hot Sprs.   39

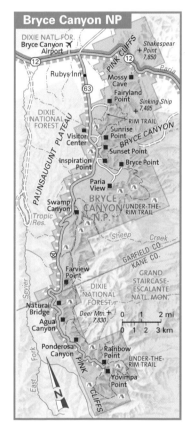

Bryce Canyon NP

DIXIE NATL. FOR.
Bryce Canyon ✈
Airport
12   12
Rubys Inn
                    Mossy
                    Cave
            Fairyland
            Point   Sinking Ship
63   + 7,405
DIXIE
NATIONAL
FOREST   RIM TRAIL
Visitor   Sunrise
Center   Point   BRYCE CANYON
Inspiration Sunset Point
Point   Bryce Point
Paria
View
Swamp   BRYCE
Canyon   CANYON   UNDER-THE-
Tropic   N.P.   RIM TRAIL
Res.
                    Sheep   Creek
                         GARFIELD CO.
                         KANE CO.
Farview   GRAND
Point   STAIRCASE-
                         ESCALANTE
          DIXIE   NATL. MON.
          NATIONAL
Natural   FOREST   Deer Mtn. +
Bridge   + 7,830
Agua   0   1   2 mi
Canyon
                   0   1   2   3 km
Ponderosa   Rainbow
Canyon   Point
            UNDER-THE-
            RIM TRAIL
            Yovimpa
            Point

PINK CLIFFS

Shakespear
+ Point
7,850

Paria

PAUNSAUGUNT PLATEAU

Sevier

East Fork

40 **Calimesa–Centerville**

Figures after entries indicate population, page number, and grid reference.

Entries in **bold black** indicate counties.
Entries in **bold color** indicate cities with detailed inset maps.

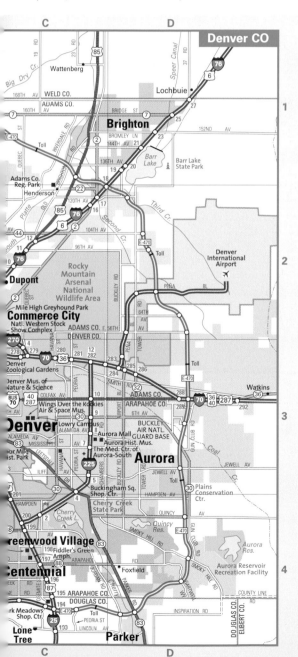

Denver CO

42 Coconino Co.–Coolidge

Figures after entries indicate population, page number, and grid reference.

POINTS OF INTEREST

Auraria Campus E2	D&F Tower F1	Post Office F1
Bus Terminal F1	Denver Art Mus. F2	Public Library F2
Byers-Evans House F2	Denver Pavilions F2	Sakura Square F1
Children's Mus. of Denver E1	Denver Performing Arts Complex ..F2	Six Flags Elitch Gardens E1
Colorado Convention Center F2	Firefighters Mus. F2	State Capitol F2
Colorado History Mus. F2	Invesco Field at Mile High E2	Tabor Center F1
Colorado's Ocean Journey E1	Larimer Square F1	Union Station F1
Coors Field F1	LoDo District F1	U.S. Court House F1
Currigan Hall F2	Metropolitan State Coll. of Denver ..E2	U.S. Mint F2
	Pepsi Center E1	Univ. of Colorado at Denver E2

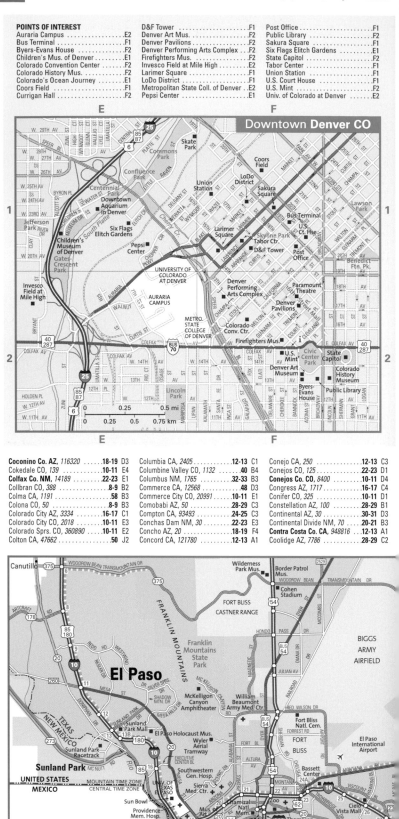

Entries in **bold black** indicate counties.
Entries in **bold color** indicate cities with detailed inset maps.

Coolidge–Fairfield **43**

El Paso TX

FORT BLISS
MILITARY
RESERVATION

44   **Fairmead–Flagler**

Figures after entries indicate population,
page number, and grid reference.

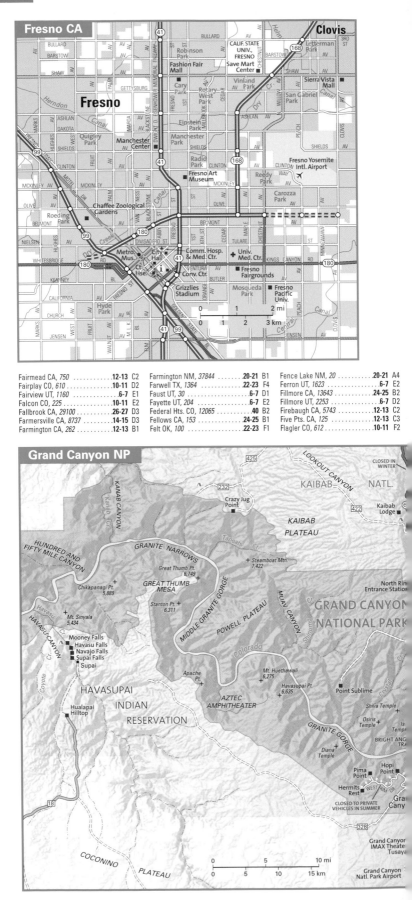

Fresno CA

Grand Canyon NP

Entries in **bold black** indicate counties.
Entries in **bold color** indicate cities with detailed inset maps.

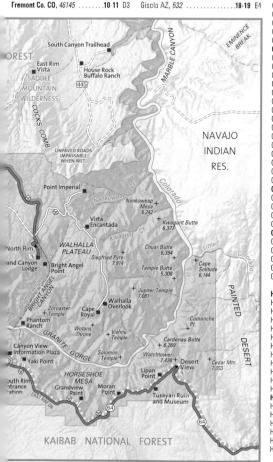

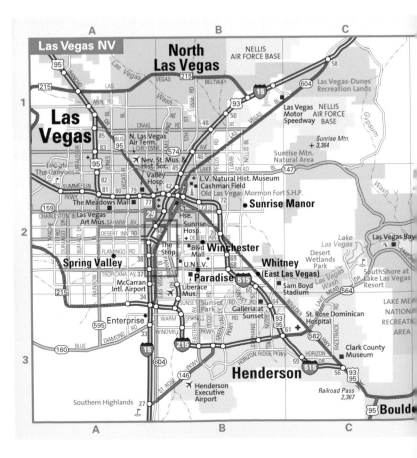

Entries in **bold black** indicate counties.
Entries in **bold color** indicate cities with detailed inset maps.

Kansas Settlement–La Cueva 47

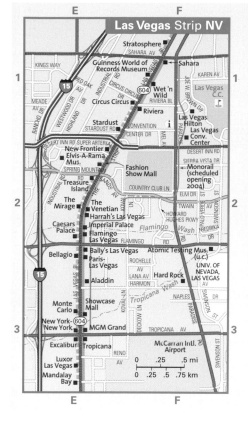

Las Vegas Strip NV

POINTS OF INTEREST

Los Angeles West CA

TRAVEL NOTE: Beginning January 2002, California started numbering freeway exits using a mileage-based numbering system. Full implementation is expected to take three years. For more details, including a complete listing of California's exit numbers, go to *www.dot.ca.gov/hq/traffops/signtech/calnexus/index.htm.*

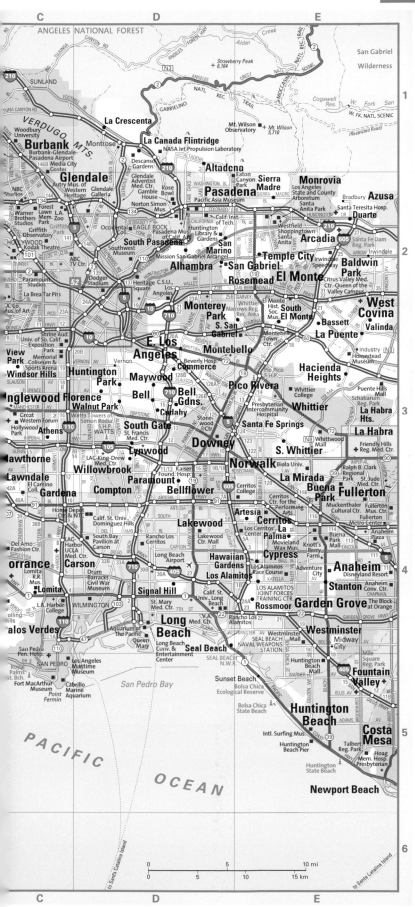

ANGELES NATIONAL FOREST

San Gabriel Wilderness

Cogswell Res.

SUNLAND

VERDUGO MTS.

La Crescenta

La Canada Flintridge

Woodbury University

Burbank

Montrose

NASA Jet Propulsion Laboratory

Mt. Wilson Observatory

Mt. Wilson 5,710

Glendale

Burbank-Glendale-Pasadena Airport

NBC Studios

Autry Mus. of Western Heritage

Glendale Galleria

Descanso Gardens

Altadena

Eaton Canyon Park

Sierra Madre

Monrovia

Azusa

Warner Brothers Studios

Forest Lawn Mem. Park

L.A. Zoo

Glendale Adventist Med. Ctr.

Rose Bowl

Pasadena

Los Angeles State and County Arboretum

Bradbury

Santa Teresita Hosp.

Duarte

Griffith Observatory

HOLLYWOOD

Kodak Theatre

Griffith Park

Norton Simon Mus.

Gamble House

Pacific Asia Museum

Santa Anita Park

Citrus Valley Med. Ctr.-Queen of the Valley Campus

Irwindale

Paramount Studios

ABC TV Ctr.

Occidental Coll.

EAGLE ROCK

Pasadena Mus. of Calif. Art

Calif. Inst. of Tech.

Westfield Shoppingtown Santa Anita

Arcadia

Irwindale Speedway

La Brea Tar Pits

Dodger Stadium

South Pasadena

Huntington Library & Gardens

San Marino

Temple City

Baldwin Park

L.A. Co. Mus. of Art

Southwest Museum

Mission San Gabriel Arcangel

Alhambra

San Gabriel

Rosemead

El Monte

West Covina

Shrine Aud.

Univ. of So. Calif.

Heritage Square

C.S.U., Los Angeles

Monterey Park

South El Monte

El Monte Hist. Soc. Mus.

Bassett

Valinda

Exposition Park

Memorial Coliseum & Sports Arena

S. San Gabriel

El Monte Narrows Rec. Area

La Puente

Industry

Homestead Museum

View Park

Windsor Hills

Huntington Park

E. Los Angeles

Montebello

Montebello Town Ctr.

Hacienda Heights

Puente Hills Mall

Vernon

Commerce

Beverly Hosp.

Pico Pico S.H.P.

Schabarum Reg. Park

Inglewood

Florence

Maywood

Bell

Bell Gdns.

Pico Rivera

Whittier College

La Habra Hts.

Hollywood Park

Athens

Walnut Park

Cudahy

Firestone

Presbyterian Intercommunity Hospital

Whittier

La Habra

Hawthorne

Willowbrook

South Gate

Stonewood

Whittwood Mall

Santa Fe Springs

Downey

S. Whittier

Friendly Hills Reg. Med. Ctr.

Lawndale

El Camino Coll.

LAC-King-Drew Med. Ctr.

Kaiser Found. Hosp.

Lynwood

Norwalk

Biola Univ.

Ralph B. Clark Regional Park

St. Jude Med. Ctr.

Gardena

Compton

Paramount

Bellflower

Cerritos College

La Mirada

Buena Park

Fullerton

Home Depot Ctr. & NTC

Calif. St. Univ. Dominguez Hills

Artesia

Cerritos

Muckenthaler Cultural Ctr.

Fullerton Mus. Ctr.

Del Amo Fashion Ctr.

South Bay Pavilion at Carson

Rancho Los Cerritos

Lakewood

Los Cerritos Center

Cerritos Ctr. for the Performing Arts

La Palma

Fullerton Metro Center

Torrance

Carson

Lakewood Ctr. Mall

Hawaiian Gardens

Movieland Wax Mus.

Cypress

Knott's Berry Farm

Buena Park Mall

Anaheim Plaza

Lomita

LAC-Harbor UCLA Med. Ctr.

Drum Barracks Civil War Museum

Long Beach Airport

Los Alamitos Race Course

Adventure City

Anaheim

Disneyland Resort

Lomita R.R. Mus.

Signal Hill

St. Mary Med. Ctr.

Los Alamitos

Los Alamitos Joint Forces Training Ctr.

Stanton

Anaheim Conv. Ctr.

Palos Verdes

WILMINGTON

L.A. Harbor College

Aquarium of the Pacific

Long Beach

V.A. Med. Ctr.

Rossmoor

Garden Grove

The Block at Orange

San Pedro Pen. Hosp.

Queen Mary

Los Angeles Maritime Museum

Long Beach Conv. & Entertainment Center

Seal Beach

Westminster Mall

Westminster

Midway City

Royal Palms St. Bch.

Fort MacArthur Museum

Cabrillo Marine Aquarium

Point Fermin

SAN PEDRO

Seal Beach N.W.R.

Sunset Beach

SEAL BEACH NAVAL WEAPONS STATION

Huntington Beach Mall

Mile Square Reg. Park

Fountain Valley

San Pedro Bay

Bolsa Chica Ecological Reserve

Bolsa Chica State Beach

Huntington Beach

Costa Mesa

Intl. Surfing Mus.

Huntington Beach Pier

Talbert Reg. Park

Hoag Mem. Hosp. Presbyterian

Huntington State Beach

PACIFIC OCEAN

Newport Beach

to Santa Catalina Island

0   5   10 mi

0   5   10   15 km

to Santa Catalina Island

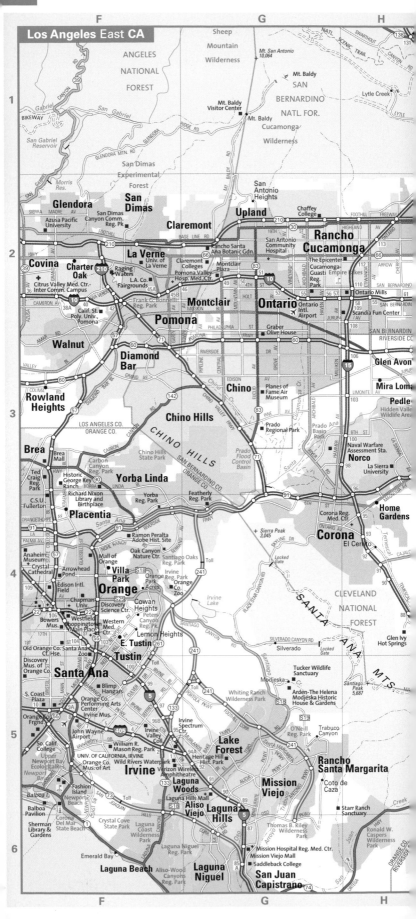

Los Angeles East CA

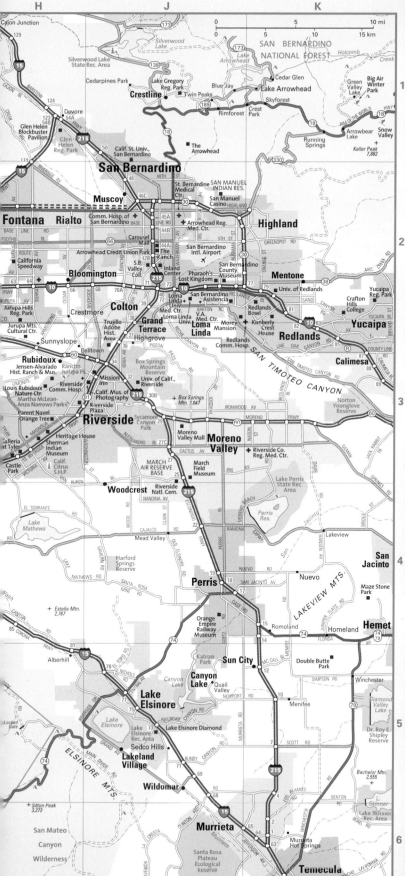

52 **Ladera Hts.–Loco Hills**

Figures after entries indicate population, page number, and grid reference.

POINTS OF INTEREST

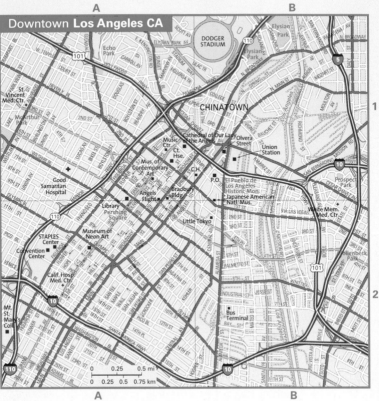

Downtown **Los Angeles CA**

Entries in **bold black** indicate counties.
Entries in **bold color** indicate cities with detailed inset maps.

Lodi–N. Edwards **53**

54 N. Fair Oaks–Panoche

Figures after entries indicate population,
page number, and grid reference.

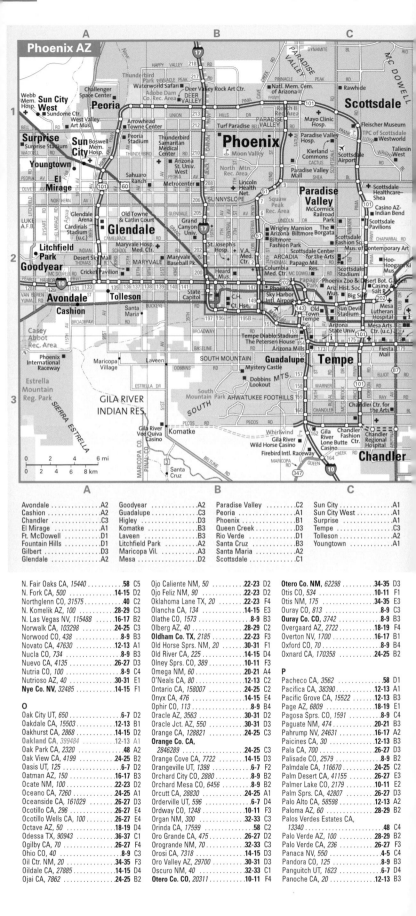

Entries in **bold black** indicate counties.
Entries in **bold color** indicate cities with detailed inset maps.

Pan Tak–Pt. Reyes Sta. 55

POINTS OF INTEREST

America West Arena F2
Arizona Center F1
Arizona Hall of Fame Mus. E2
Arizona Mining & Mineral Mus. . .E2
Arizona Science Center F2
Arizona State Capitol E2

Arizona State Fairgrounds E1
Arizona Veterans Mem. Coliseum E1
Bank One Ballpark F2
Bus Terminal F2
City Hall E2
Civic Plaza F2
Court House E2

Heard Mus. F1
Herberger Theater Center F2
Heritage Square F2
Phoenix Art Mus. E1
Phoenix Mus. of Hist. F2
Union Station E2
U.S. Court House E2

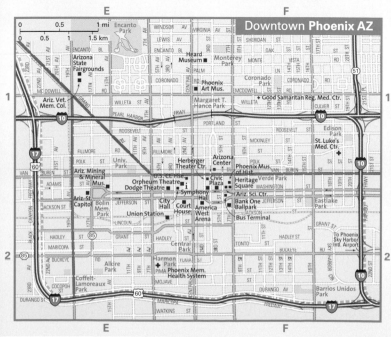

Downtown **Phoenix AZ**

56 Pojoaque–Randsburg

Figures after entries indicate population,
page number, and grid reference.

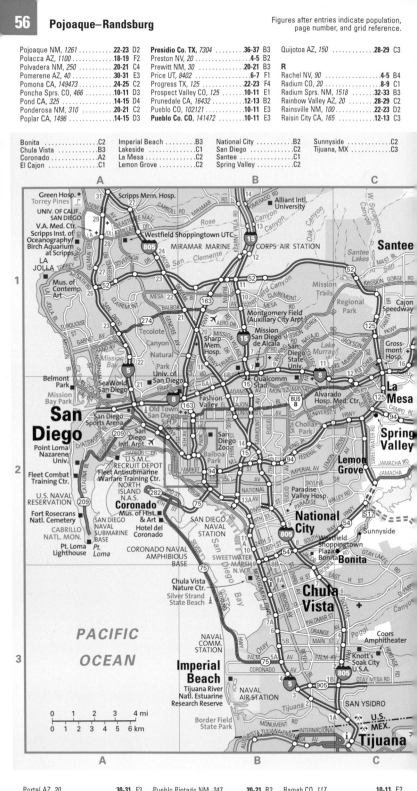

Entries in **bold black** indicate counties.
Entries in **bold color** indicate cities with detailed inset maps.

Rangely–Roll 57

POINTS OF INTEREST

Automotive Mus. E1
Balboa Park E1
Balboa Stadium E2
Ballpark (u.c.) E2
Casa del Prado E1
Children's Mus. D2
City Hall D2
Civic Center D2
Copley Symphony Hall E2
County Court House D2
Cruise Ship Terminal D2
Edison Centre for the Performing Arts ...E1
Firehouse Mus. D2
Fleet & Industrial Supply Center D2
Gaslamp Quarter & W. H. Davis House ...D2
Horton Plaza D2
House of Hospitality E1
Maritime Mus. D2

Mus. of Contemporary Art, Downtown D2
Reuben H. Fleet Space Theater &
　Science Center E1
San Diego Aerospace Mus. E1
San Diego Convention Center D2
San Diego Intl. Arpt. (Lindbergh Field) D1
San Diego Mus. of Art E1
San Diego Museum of Man E1
San Diego National Hist. Mus. E1
San Diego Zoo E1
Santa Fe Station D2
Seaport Village D2
Spanish Village Art Center E1
Sports Mus. E1
Spreckels Organ Pavilion E1
Starlight Bowl E1
Timken Mus. of Art E1
U.S. Court House D2

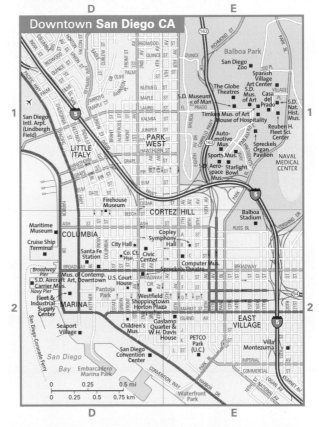

Downtown San Diego CA

58

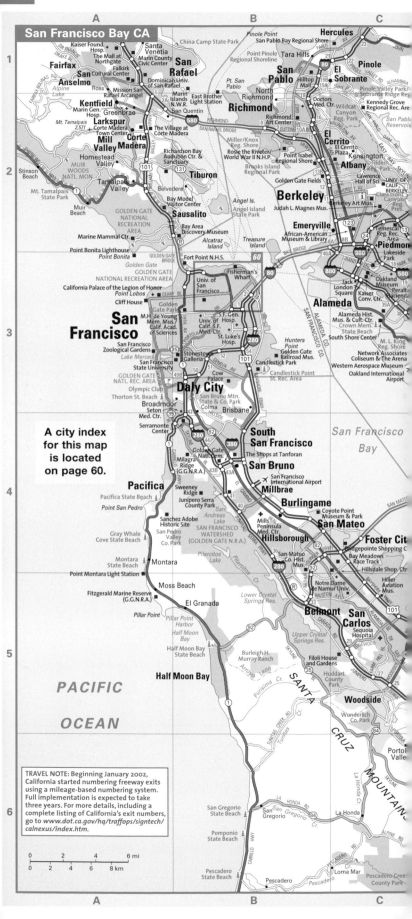

A city index
for this map
is located
on page 60.

PACIFIC

OCEAN

TRAVEL NOTE: Beginning January 2002,
California started numbering freeway exits
using a mileage-based numbering system.
Full implementation is expected to take
three years. For more details, including a
complete listing of California's exit numbers,
go to *www.dot.ca.gov/hq/traffops/signtech/
calnexus/index.htm.*

0   2   4   6 mi
0   2   4   6   8 km

Labels on map

Pinole Point
China Camp State Park
Hercules
Point Pinole
Regional Shoreline
Pinole Bay Regional Shore
Tara Hills
Pinole
El
Sobrante
Kaiser Found.
Hosp.
Santa
Venetia
Marin County
Civic Center
San
Rafael
Pt. San
Pablo
San
Pablo
Hilltop
Mall
Pinole Valley Park/
Sobrante Ridge Reg
Kennedy Grove
Regional Rec. Are
Fairfax
The Mall at
Northgate
Falkirk
Cultural Center
Dominican
Univ.
of San Rafael
North
Richmond
Doctors
Med. Ctr.
Wildcat
Canyon
Reg. Park
San
Anselmo
Ross
Mission San
Rafael Arcangel
Marin
Islands
N.W.R.
East Brother
Light Station
Richmond
Richmond
Art Center
El
Cerrito
El Cerrito
Plaza
San Pablo
Reservoir
Kentfield
Marin Gen.
Hosp.
Greenbrae
San Quentin
Kensington
Larkspur
Corte Madera
Town Center
The Village at
Corte Madera
Miller/Knox
Reg. Shore.
Rosie the Riveter/
World War II N.H.P.
Lawrence
Hall of Sci.
Mill
Valley
Corte
Madera
Richardson Bay
Audubon Ctr. &
Sanctuary
Point Isabel
Regional Shore
Berkeley Art Mus.
Homestead
Valley
Tiburon
Brooks Island
Regional Park
Golden Gate Fields
Berkeley
Stinson
Beach
Tamalpais
Valley
Belvedere
Golden Gate Fields
Judah L. Magnes Mus.
Mt. Tamalpais
State Park
Muir
Beach
Bay Model
Visitor Center
Angel Is.
Angel Island
State Park
Emeryville
African-American
Museum & Library
Sausalito
Treasure
Island
Marine Mammal Ctr.
Bay Area
Discovery Museum
Alcatraz
Island
Piedmon
Lakeside
Park
Point Bonita Lighthouse
Point Bonita
Fort Point N.H.S.
Oakland
Museum
Kaiser
Conv. Ctr.
California Palace of the Legion of Honor
Point Lobos
Univ.
of San
Francisco
Fisherman's
Wharf
Jack
London
Square
Alameda
Cliff House
Golden
Gate Park
S.F. Gen.
Hosp.
Alameda Hist.
Mus. & Cult. Ctr.
San
Francisco
M.H. de Young
Mem. Mus./
Calif. Acad.
of Sciences
Univ. of
Calif. S.F.
Med. Ctr.
St. Luke's
Hosp.
Crown Mem.
State Beach
South Shore Center
San Francisco
Zoological Gardens
Stonestown
Galleria
Hunters
Point
Golden Gate
Railroad Mus.
M. L. King
Reg. Shore.
San Francisco
State University
Cow
Palace
Candlestick Park
Network Associates
Coliseum & The Arena
Western Aerospace Museum
Lake Merced
Olympic Club
Daly City
Candlestick Point
St. Rec. Area
Oakland International
Airport
Thorton St. Beach
Broadmoor
Seton
Med. Ctr.
San Bruno Mtn.
State & Co. Park
Colma
Brisbane
**San Francisco
Bay**
Serramonte
Center
South
San Francisco
Pacifica
Golden Gate
Natl. Cem.
The Shops at Tanforan
Milagra
Ridge
(G.G.N.R.A.)
San Bruno
Pacifica State Beach
Sweeney
Ridge
Junipero Serra
County Park
San Francisco
International Airport
Point San Pedro
Millbrae
Sanchez Adobe
Historic Site
San Pedro
Valley
Co. Park
San
Andreas
Lake
Burlingame
Gray Whale
Cove State Beach
Coyote Point
Museum & Park
Mills
Peninsula
Med. Ctr.
San Mateo
Montara
State Beach
Montara
San Francisco
Watershed
(Golden Gate N.R.A.)
Hillsborough
Foster Cit
Bridgepointe Shopping C
Point Montara Light Station
Pilarcitos
Lake
San Mateo
Co. Hist.
Mus.
Bay Meadows
Race Track
Fitzgerald Marine Reserve
(G.G.N.R.A.)
El Granada
Hillsdale Shop. Ce
Pillar Point
Lower Crystal
Springs Res.
Notre Dame
de Namur Univ.
Hiller
Aviation
Mus.
Pillar Point
Harbor
Half Moon
Bay
Belmont
San
Carlos
Half Moon Bay
State Beach
Upper Crystal
Springs Res.
Sequoia
Hospital
Half Moon Bay
Burleigh H.
Murray Ranch
Filoli House
and Gardens
Huddart
County
Park
Woodside
Wunderlich
Co. Park
Portol
Valle
San Gregorio
State Beach
San
Gregorio
La Honda
Loma Mar
Pomponio
State Beach
Pescadero
State Beach
Pescadero
Pescadero Cree
County Park

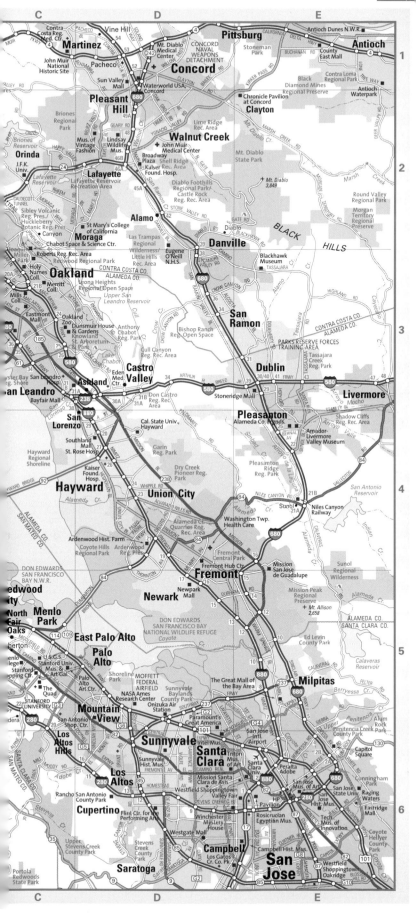

San Francisco City Index

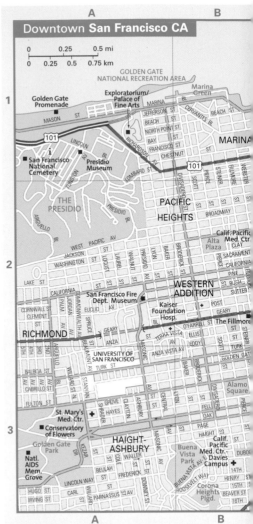

Downtown San Francisco CA

POINTS OF INTEREST

Entries in **bold black** indicate counties.
Entries in **bold color** indicate cities with detailed inset maps.

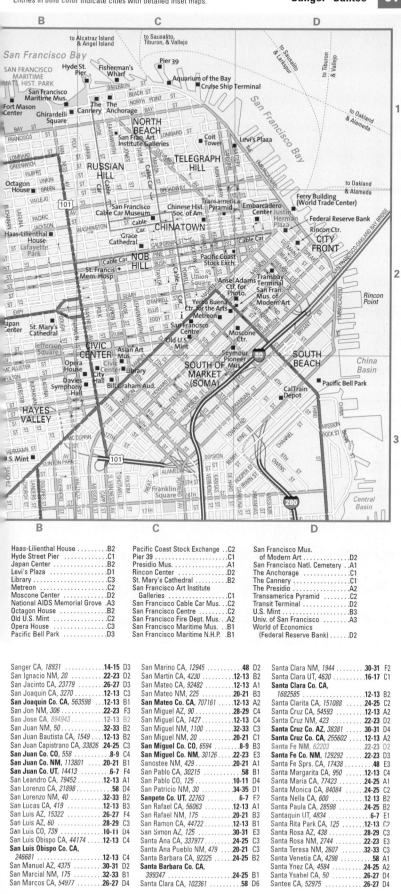

62 **Santo Domingo Pueblo–Somis**

Figures after entries indicate population, page number, and grid reference.

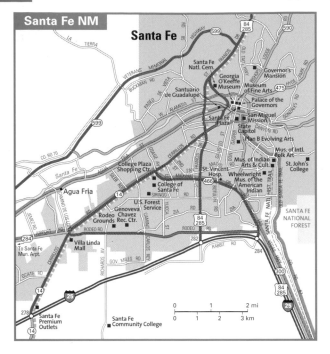

Santa Fe NM

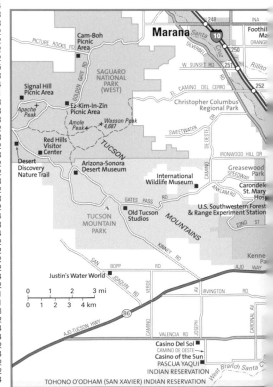

Entries in **bold black** indicate counties.
Entries in **bold color** indicate cities with detailed inset maps.

Sonoita–Towaoc 63

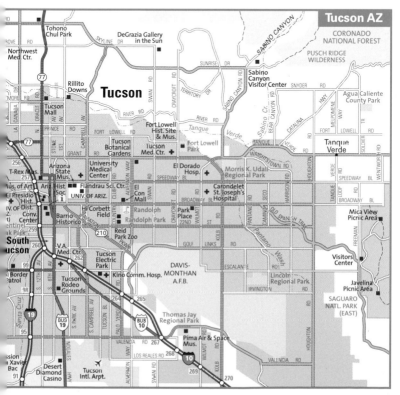

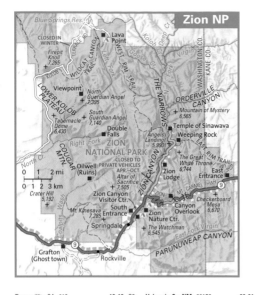

Zion NP

Blue Springs Res.
CLOSED IN WINTER
Lava Point
Firepit Knoll 7,265
Viewpoint
North Guardian Angel 7,395
South Guardian Angel 7,140
Double Falls
Tabernacle Dome 6,430
Angels Landing 5,900
Temple of Sinawava
Weeping Rock
ZION NATIONAL PARK
CLOSED TO PRIVATE VEHICLES APR-OCT
Oilwell (Ruins)
The Great White Throne 6,744
Altar of Sacrifice 7,505
Zion Lodge
East Entrance
Zion Canyon Visitor Ctr.
Checkerboard Mesa 6,670
Canyon Overlook
Mt. Khesava 7,285
South Entrance
Zion Nature Ctr.
Crater Hill 5,192
Springdale
The Watchman 6,545
Grafton (Ghost town)
Rockville
PARUNUWEAP CANYON
East Fork Virgin
0 1 2 mi
0 1 2 3 km
Blue Springs Res.
LOWER KOLOB PLATEAU
WIDCAT CANYON
KOLOB CANYON
THE NARROWS
ORDERVILLE CANYON
Mountain of Mystery 6,565
WASHINGTON CO.
KANE CO.
COUGAR MTN.
ZION CANYON
EAST RIM TRAIL
MT. CARMEL HWY.
9